new housing concepts

Mahler, Gunster & Fuchs Wilhelm Hu
Architects Ignacio Vicens & Jose Antonio
Toyo Ito Klaus Kada Soisick Cleret Thierr
Fauconnet & Leopold Arkkitehtitoimisto M
Wiel Arets Toshio Akimoto Massimiliano
Architects Francis Soler Carlo
Burkhalter Splittewerk Dietric
Carlo Baumschlager & Die
Jean Nouvel Philippe Gaz
Hauvette Herzog & De
Beat Consoni Hel
Wolff-Plottegg
Architectuur st
Mike Guyer D
Architectuur Cla
& Schulze Arc
Kollhoff Legorr
Bonell, Brull

r & Enrich **Kessler** Erick Van Egeraat

mos Nickl & Partner architekten **MVRDV**

Nabères & Jacques **Fourcade** Magendie,

Ò Josep Lluís Mateo & Jaume Avellaneda

ksas Architecture Studio V.P. Tuominen

Ferrater **Christian Sumi & Marianne**

Fink & Thomas Jocher Hermann & Bosch

ar Eberle **Shigeru Ban Alsop & Stormer**

Philippe Madec Eduard Broto Christian

euron Josep Lluís Mateo W.J. Neutelings

& Siitonen **Santiago Calatrava** Manfred

hn Fischer & Partner Frank O. Gehry

ò Herman Hertzberger Annette Gigon &

ozer König Architects W.J. Neutelings

& Kaan **Maccreanor & Lavington** Geurst

ten **Schmidt, Hammer & Lassen** Hans

Arquitectos K. Nikolaidis & C. Edwards

Gil & Rius.

Work conception: **Carles Broto**
Publisher: **Arian Mostaedi**

Graphic design & production: **Francisco Orduña**

ISBN: 84-89861-20-X
D.L.: B-21138/00

Printed in Spain

new housing concepts

leadinginternational
publishing group

Introduction

The typology of collective housing has undergone major transformations in the course of the 20th century. The postulates of the Modern Movement, which involved a radical change in the conception of the habits of life and in the organisation of residential architecture during the first half of the 20th century, led to the development of new proposals for collective housing. The ideal pursued was that of a healthy dwelling in a happy world, a scenario for life and for new forms of coexistence that reinforced the community feeling among its inhabitants without forcing them to give up their independence.

Though we are now on the threshold of the 21st century, it cannot be said that the objectives of this ambitious enterprise have been achieved. The economic growth that took place in a large part of the world after the Second World War led to the creation of mass housing programmes governed by the laws of speculation and lacking planning, which not only made our cities ugly but also contributed greatly to the degradation of the life of their inhabitants. Furthermore, the avant-garde experiments that pursued a scientific reformulation of society and the city through architecture have in most of the cases proven to be failures.

It is therefore not surprising that though architects feel an understandable disenchantment with the knowledge of how much remains to be done, there is a favourable climate for reflection and invention. Numerous conditions affect the residential typology and raise challenges that are often difficult to solve. Factors such as scale, services, local regulations, budget cuts or typological and formal demands of clients are only a few of the limitations that force architects to work in a very narrow margin of action and make it difficult to offer audacious solutions to the changing needs that have arisen in the last few years.

The standards that govern housing are out of date, far from the real demands of their residents. Nevertheless, architects still find the dwelling a fascinating subject. The possibility of designing an inhabitable space, of creating an environment in which a group of people live and interact, is a challenge that few professionals can resist. Whether it is a residential complex or a vertical dwelling, a public or a private initiative, a building aimed at a heterogeneous public or at a community with special needs (students, workers, the elderly, etc.), each scheme must ensure that its inhabitants can create their own safe and comfortable space: a home.

The projects in this volume illustrate the latest tendencies in collective housing. They include both large and small-scale residential projects that share a common spirit: they are rigorous and imaginative proposals that give priority to the inhabitants and use the environment in which they are located as a framework for defining them and giving them meaning; attractive and functional solutions conceived by architects who are highly committed to current trends. Under the apparent diversity of these proposals there is an underlying desire to give the housing space dynamism and personality, to make each housing unit mould itself to its occupants so that they can transform it at will. Another characteristic common to most projects is the use of simple materials —often those found in the architectural tradition of the area— and pragmatic and economic construction solutions. In the works of architects such as Frank O. Gehry, Santiago Calatrava, Jean Nouvel, Massimiliano Fuksas, Toshio Akimoto and Wiel Arets, to name just a few of the famous and emerging architects included in this book, we can find stimulating answers, ingenious solutions, unexpected points of view and proposals that will without doubt influence the conception of residential architecture in the century to come.

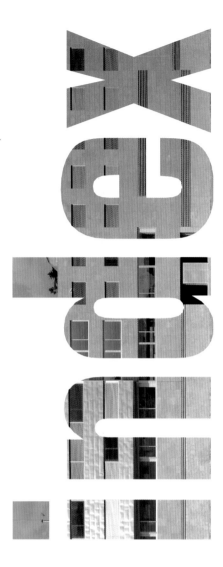

Mahler, Günster & Fuchs
Residence in the Black Forest
Neuenbürg, Germany

Situated on the banks of the River Enz, this complex of 28 dwellings is articulated into four almost identical blocks that reflect the scale of the urban environment. Set out neatly in a row, they are rectangular in plan and have their short ends parallel to the river. The order allows them to pick up some of the grain of the village, where houses have traditionally turned their gables towards the bank to allow access to the water.

The new four-storey buildings, covered from ground to eaves in ship-lap timber boarding, have the workmanlike neatness and directness of the Functional Tradition. Their large external sliding shutters add to the impression and they appear from a distance to be barns of some sort, or rather old-fashioned warehouses. Closer inspection reveals that they do in fact contain flats, and detailed examination shows that this is housing for the elderly. 20 of the dwellings are for one-person occupancy and the others for two people; areas range from 45sqm to 53sqm.

The basic block arrangement is very simple: flats are arranged in pairs on each floor; upper levels are reached from timber access galleries on the long north-east sides which are served by lifts and stairs; on the opposite side, generous balconies open to the sun. Individual flats are simple and quite small: they have a living area as the centre of activity; off this are the kitchen recess and the sleeping alcove (in many units, there are separate bedrooms).

A solar energy system was incorporated into the scheme. It provides hot water and also supports the heating. In order to integrate the collectors into the south-west-facing roof slopes, the roofs were covered with corrugated perspex sheets. The high transmission value of this material ensures a great degree of efficiency. The transparency of the external skin also allows the geometry of the timber structure to be seen, even in the roof. The attic space itself is unheated and accommodates services and storage areas.

Photographs: Christian Richters

The residential complex is articulated by means of the alignment of four identical rectangular blocks oriented so that on the shortest side they are parallel to the river Enz.

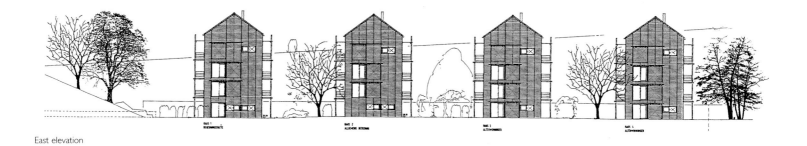

East elevation

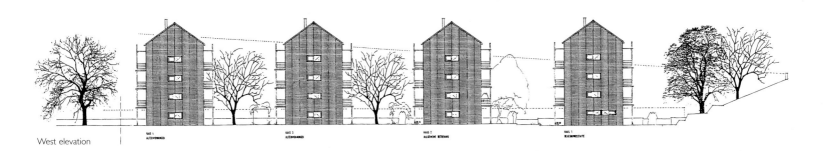

West elevation

The openings are protected from the strong sunlight by large sliding shutters. As can be seen on the following page, to reduce the energy consumption of the dwellings, the south-west slope of the roof has been clad with solar panels of transparent corrugated perspex.

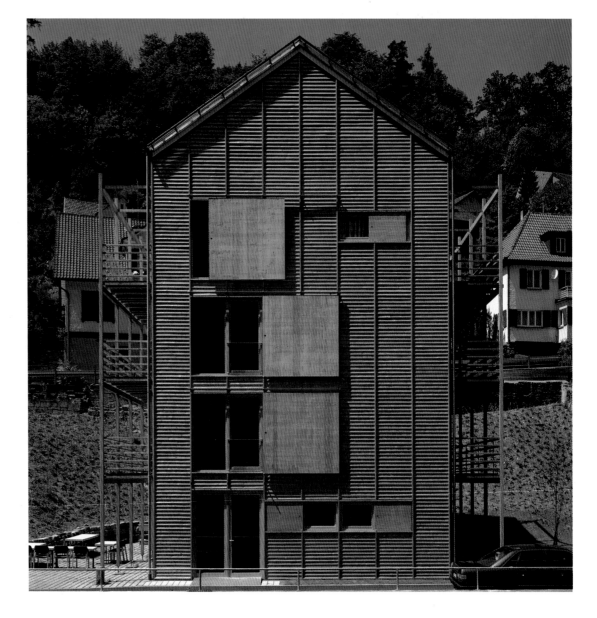

Upper level floor plan

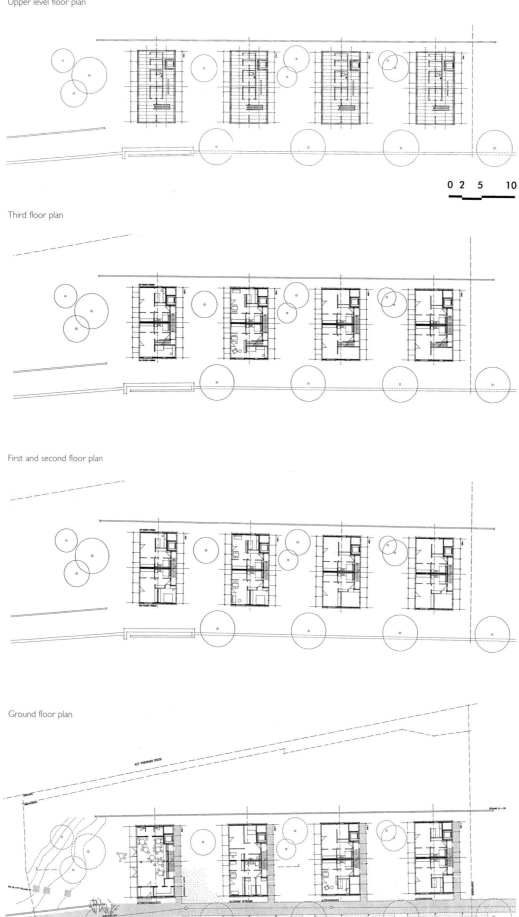

0 2 5 10

Third floor plan

First and second floor plan

Ground floor plan

14

The buildings have a reinforced concrete structure and have been clad with untreated pine so that their colour turns gray with the passing of time.

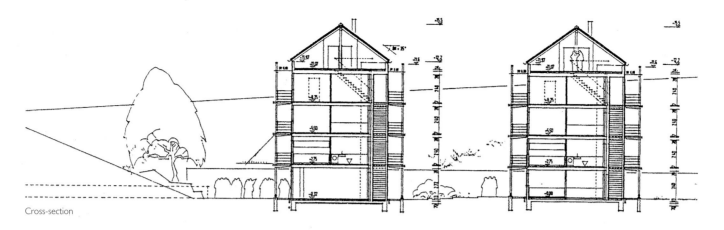

Cross-section

Wilhelm Huber & Erich Kessler

Housing for the elderly

Eichstätt, Germany

The historic city outline shows a homogeneous structure on the western edge bordering on the Altmühl. The new development reflects the layout of a former abattoir on this site.

The long, straight roof line, on the other hand, stands in contrast to the roofscape of the old city centre. A rupture in the building volume allows views of the Altmühl on one side and of the old town on the other side. The project included the rehabilitation of the adjoining historic Jura House to provide additional accommodation in the form of several old apartments after minor conversions.

Some of the features of the older building, such as the solid external wall construction punctured by window openings, were adopted in the new design. The loggias and living room windows facing the river can be darkened by closing perforated metal sliding screens. The aspect facing the town is distinguished by the timber stores in front of the flats, by the generous access balconies and by the broad roof projection at the top.

Photographs: Peter Bonfig

Located at the edge of the historic city, the old people's resi-dence faces the river Altmühl on the west side.

The linearity of the walkways that give access to the dwellings is interrupted by the placing of a series of small box rooms that are totally clad in wood.

On the side that opens up toward the town, the building is char-acter-ized by its wide access walkways to the dwellings and its generous, overhanging roof.

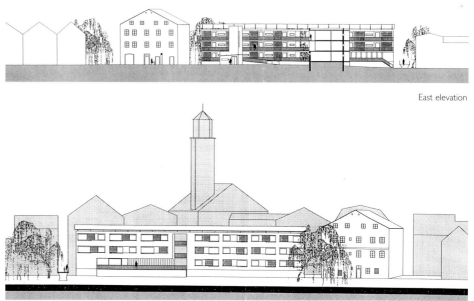

East elevation

West elevation

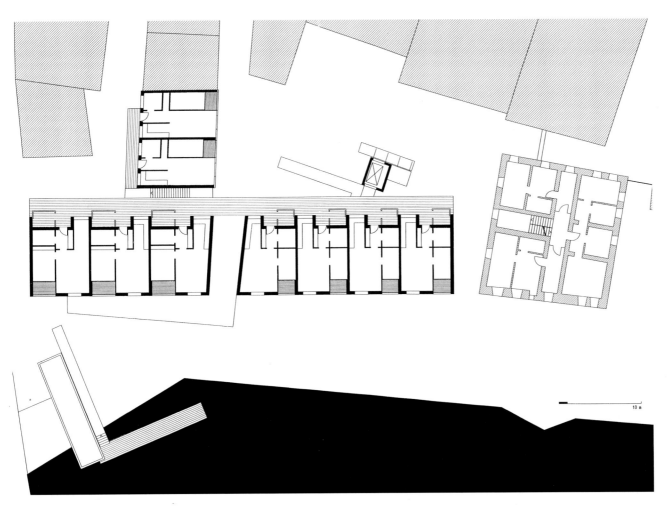

Typical floor plan

Ground floor plan

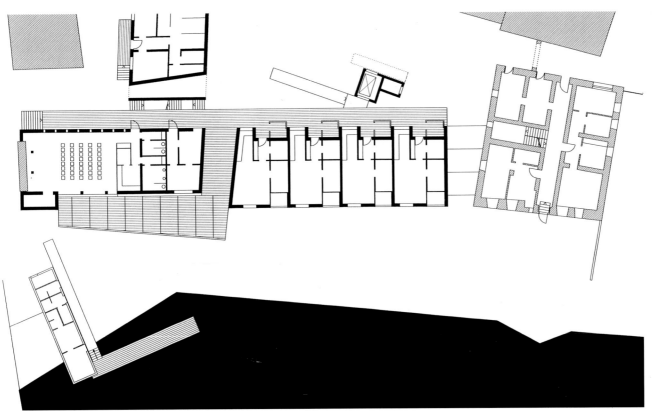

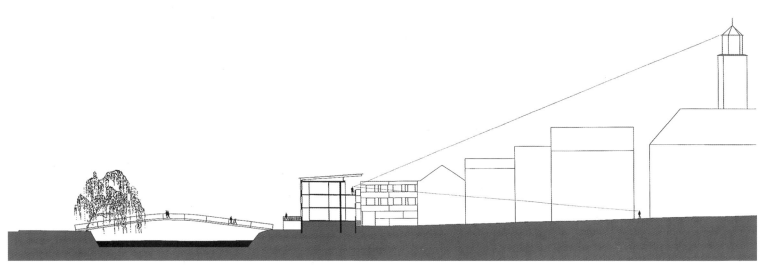

Cross section

As can be seen in the photograph on the left, the west facade filters the incoming light by means of a system of sliding panels of perforated metal.

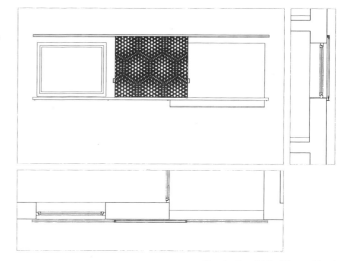

Construction detail of the west facade

Erick van Egeraat Architects

Housing for Seniors

Niejmegen, The Netherlands

The Dobbelmanweg in Nijmegen used to house a monumental complex dating from the beginning of this century, comprising a church, a monastery and a school. The church and the former monastery with its garden have been retained in the project; the school made way for a housing complex, located on the border of the old cemetery.

The monastery-garden and the cemetery formed the leading theme for the project. A modern solution was chosen for the building, which opposes any form of nostalgia. In order for the green courtyard to be accessible, a pedestrian through-road has been created from the Dobbelmanweg, following the cemetery to the Hindestraat. A lift has been integrated into the project to guarantee optimum accessibility. The block consists of 24 three-room dwellings of different types and volumes. In the longitudinal section, the block is bent twice to make a good connection with the existing buildings. Most of the houses have a view

onto the green area. The dwellings at the head of the block have a view of the Dobbelmanweg. On the south side, the galleries have been staggered over the upper dwelling levels. The dwellings at ground level have their own entrance from a raised gallery on the north side and their own (small) garden on the south side. A communal garden for all inhabitants can also be found on the south side. This garden can be reached through the gallery or the main entrance.

The dwellings have been designed with an open floor plan. Most important was to realise two bedrooms of equal quality in each apartment. The two bedrooms are separated by open cupboard units, which can be used in just one of the bedrooms. It is simple to adapt the house to the specific wishes of the inhabitants, as the separation walls can be moved without radical intervention. Each house has a direct connection between the living room and the kitchen.

Photographs: Christian Richters

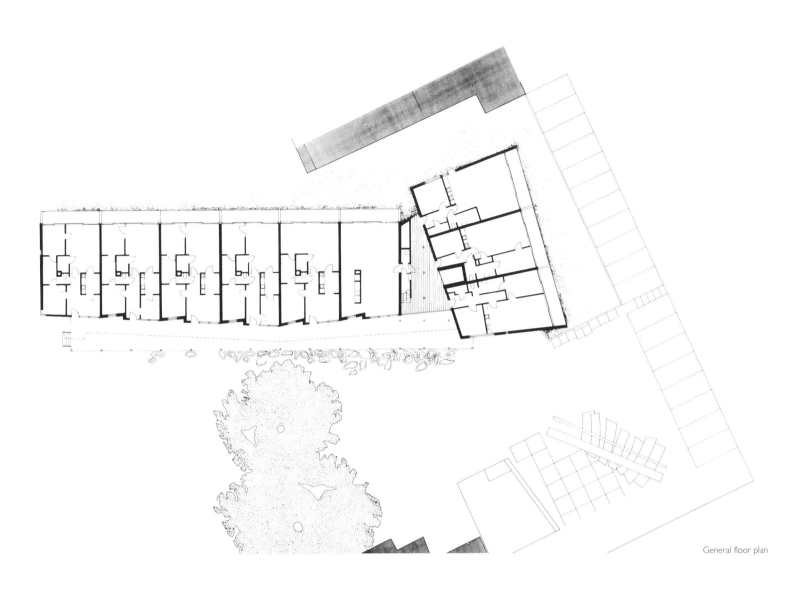

General floor plan

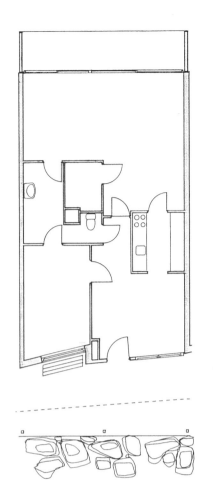

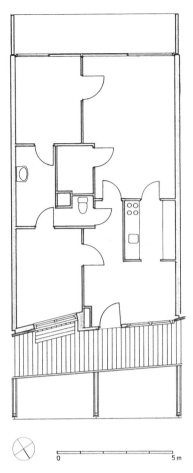

Ground floor plan

First floor plan

0   5 m

The housing block, which only has three floors, has 24 three-bedroom apartments of different volumes and types. A lift has been installed in order to give greater accessibility to the whole building.
In the residential block, most of the apartments give onto the green area, thus providing greater quality of life.

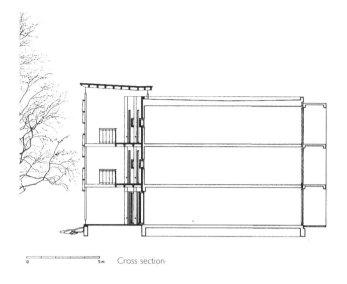

0 ___ 5m   Cross section

The dwellings on the ground floor have
their own access from the raised gallery
and also have a small private garden.

The architectural solution and the materials that have been chosen for this intervention avoid any type of nostalgic form, adopting a clearly modern language.

Ignacio Vicens & José Antonio Ramos

Asilo de Ancianos

Alcázar de San Juan, Spain

The site is located in an industrial area on the outskirts of town at the point of contact between the city and the country, thus offering the possibility of defining its own environment. A longitudinal layout of parallel wings is proposed, perforated by multiple openings onto courtyards and gardens. In such a clearly longitudinal layout the transverse views and perspectives create a special tension, and the clarity of the layout contrasts with the functional complexities of the internal organisation.

The treatment of the external walls, rendered in cement oxidised with iron sulphate, reveals the will to integrate its volumes into an environment of reddish terrain. This same will can be seen in the design of the gardens, which exclusively use local elements.

The emphasis in the interconnection of exterior and interior spaces leads to the treatment of the gardens as a fundamental part of the space for the use of the elderly.

The olive trees mark places of rest and meeting in the garden, while the more protected spaces of the porches in double and triple height are underlined in their verticality by the cypress trees. The living rooms are perforated with large windows that open onto courtyards with fountains and ponds.

The garden and building are intoned with the colours of the land and the surrounding vegetation. The interior spaces are articulated by ramps and walkways, which offer a spatial fluidity that belies the rigid ground plan. Here natural light is used to underline the space. In the chapel the light sources are deep and excavated in the walls, underlining their thickness; also, their situation in the corners helps to define the space volumetrically and to define it as a unitary whole. The incorporation of the private chapel of the nuns in the volume of the church gives spatial and thematic order to the spaces devoted to worship and prayer.

Photographs: Eugeni Pons

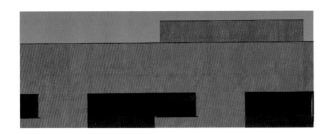

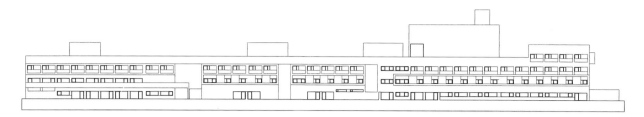

South elevation

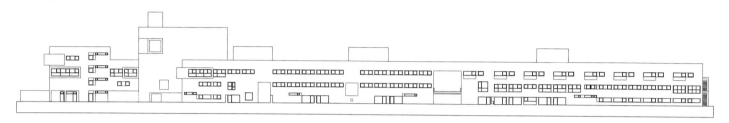

North elevation

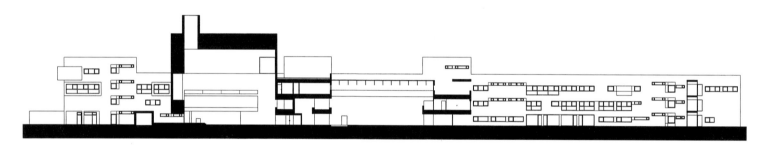

Longitudinal section

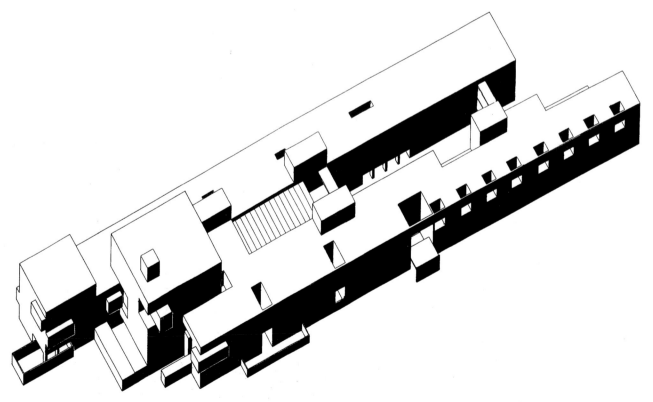

Axonometric projection

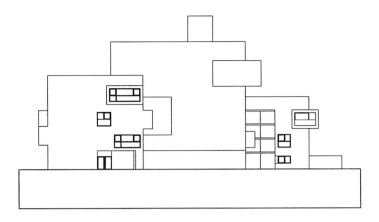

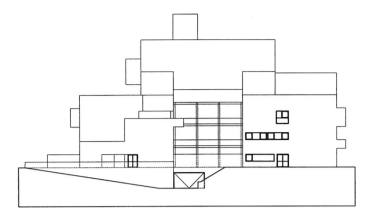

East elevation

West elevation

Aluminium joinery with a black veneer contrasts with the surface finish of the exterior walls, which have been fixed using oxidised concrete with iron sulphate. Thus, we see the firm will of the architects to integrate the building into a landscape dominated by the colour of deep red earth.

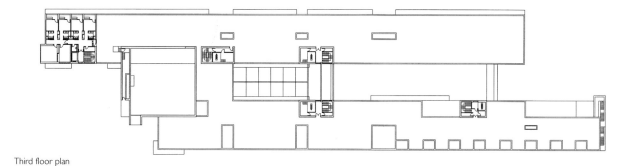

Third floor plan

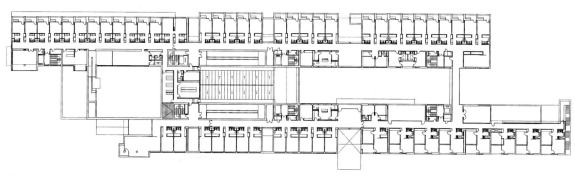

Second floor plan

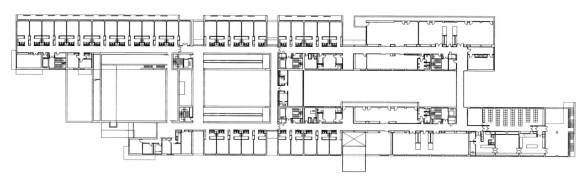

First floor plan

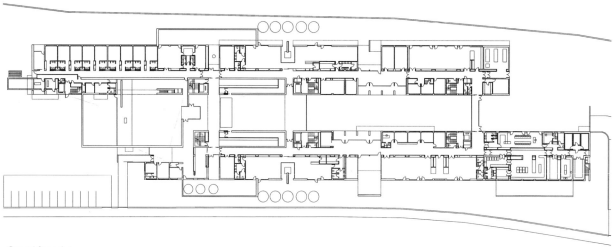

Ground floor plan

The linearity of the design is further enhanced by the irregular arrangement of geometric perforations in the walls which mark circulation spaces. These perforations also contribute to a better diffusion of light.

Nickl & Partner architekten
Hospital and Old People's Centre

Beilngries, Germany

Designed as a model project, this complex comprises a hospital, an old people's home, a nursing home for the elderly, as well as old people's and staff dwellings, all united in a single building.

The development is situated in a dominant urban position not far from the old, walled town centre.

The ensemble consists of a newly refurbished classicistic building that had undergone major alterations in the 1960's and a new structure of similar size.

The two sections are set at an angle to each other. This layout allowed the creation of a generous central stair case space lit by a large top light and by windows at the side. This space is located immediately next to the main entrance and provides access to all areas.

The coloration of the exposed concrete soffits around the light-well openings ranges from a bold blue through light red to bright yellow. Colours also play an important role in the façade design.

The slightly set-back main entrance forms the junction between the old and new sections of the building. It functions as a wind lobby with sliding doors in a glass and metal façade. The entrance canopy is suspended at the sides form the two building tracts set at an angle to each other. Only the rainwater gutter is fixed directly to the actual entrance façade.

The canopy consists of alternate areas of transparent glass and opaque yellow fibre-cement slabs, resulting in a gradual diminution of brightness from outside to inside.

Photographs: Dieter Leistner / Architekton

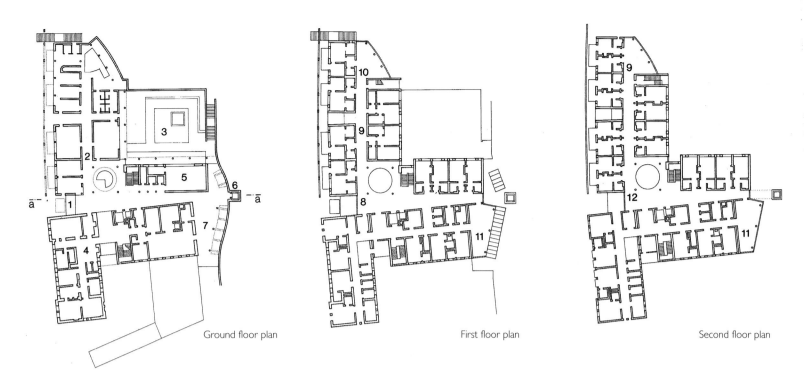

Ground floor plan   First floor plan   Second floor plan

1.Lobby. 2.Physiotherapy. 3.Recreation area. 4.Medical department. 5.Chapel. 6.Lift to park. 7.Dining room. 8.Infirmary. 9.Bedrooms. 10.Therapy station. 11.Lounge. 12.Nursing ward

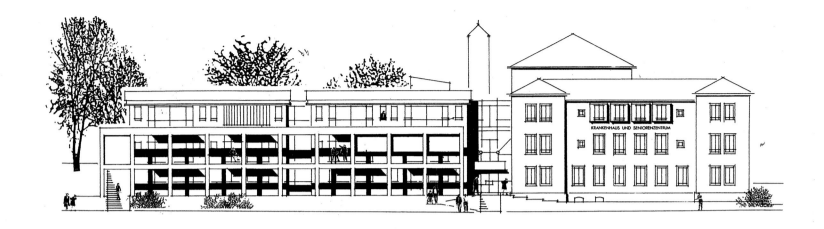

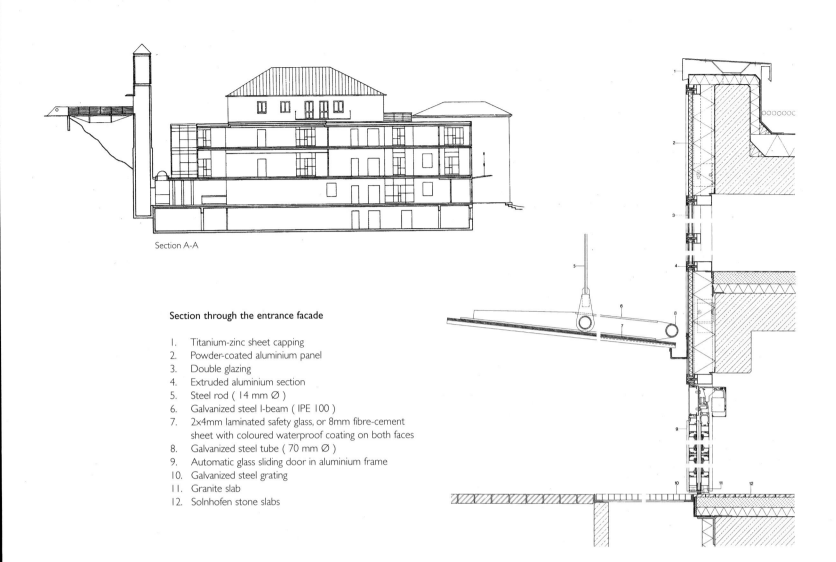

Section A-A

Section through the entrance facade

1. Titanium-zinc sheet capping
2. Powder-coated aluminium panel
3. Double glazing
4. Extruded aluminium section
5. Steel rod (14 mm Ø)
6. Galvanized steel I-beam (IPE 100)
7. 2×4mm laminated safety glass, or 8mm fibre-cement
   sheet with coloured waterproof coating on both faces
8. Galvanized steel tube (70 mm Ø)
9. Automatic glass sliding door in aluminium frame
10. Galvanized steel grating
11. Granite slab
12. Solnhofen stone slabs

The interior walls of exposed concrete have a varnished finish in different tones that range from bright blue to brilliant yellow to luminous red.

The project consists in restoring the existing building and building a similar structure that allows the services of the complex to be extended. At the point where these two bodies converge, both in L-shape, a wide nucleus of vertical communication is located. It is near the main entrance, thus facilitating access to any area of the centre, and it is toplit through a large skylight.

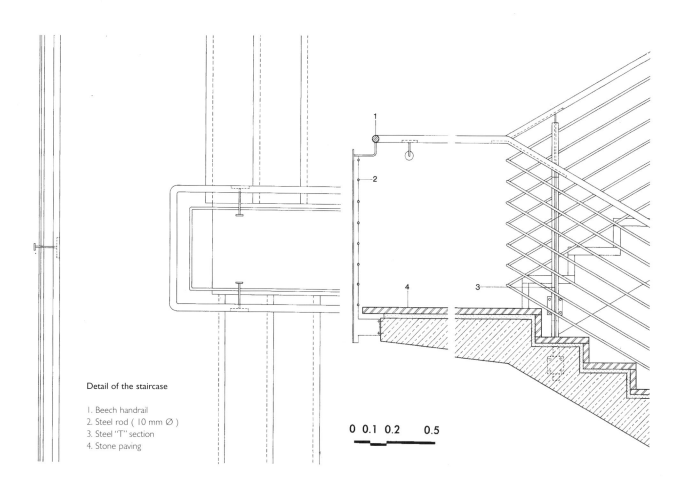

Detail of the staircase

1. Beech handrail
2. Steel rod (10 mm Ø)
3. Steel "T" section
4. Stone paving

0 0.1 0.2   0.5

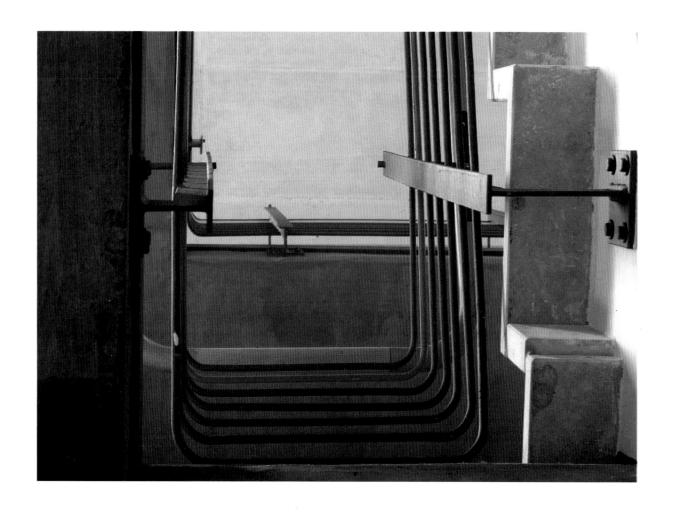

MVRDV

100 Wozoco's

Amsterdam-Osdorp, The Netherlands

A block of 100 apartments for persons over 50 years of age was to be built in a garden city situated in the west of Amsterdam (Westelijke Tuinsteden), an area whose green spaces are threatened with continually increasing occupation density. The apartments were to offer a higher degree of independence than is usual in homes for the elderly, and could in the future also accommodate younger residents. The current zoning envelope and the north-south orientation of the building made it impossible to distribute the 100 apartments in a single block, which could only take 87. The remaining 13 were suspended from the north facade of the block using steel cantilever girders, in such a way that each hanging apartment receives the sun on its east or west facade (in the Netherlands, it is not permitted to build north-facing apartments). The overhanging units placed along the north facade give it a striking presence in the street

and the east-west orientation of these units combines with the north-south orientation of the apartments in the interior of the block.

Each gallery of the block has a different perspective, and the different window positions, balcony sizes and balcony materials give the flats their own character. For sound insulation, the party walls were built 8 cm thicker than was structurally necessary, and this extra thickness was used to connect the cantilever trusses without having to increase the weight of the load-bearing walls. Sound and fire regulations made it necessary to clad these trusses.

The solution to this project means that the ground floor spaces characteristic of these neighbourhoods are left as open and green as possible, and a prototypical increase in density is achieved for this area.

Photographs: Christian Richters

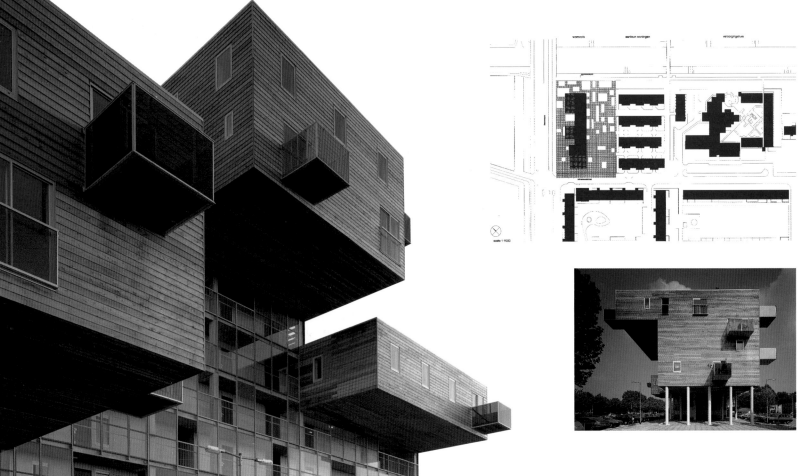

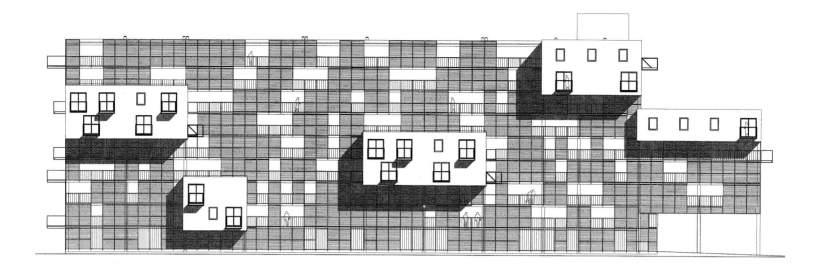

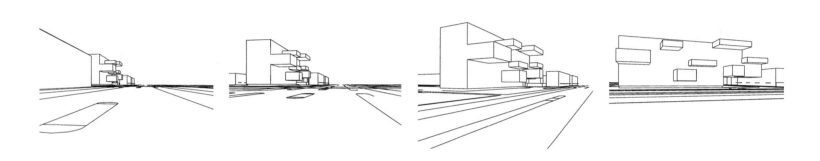

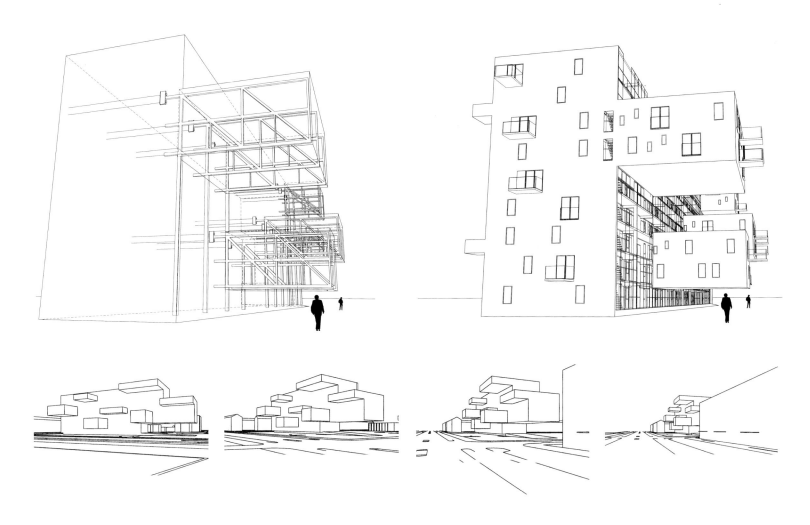

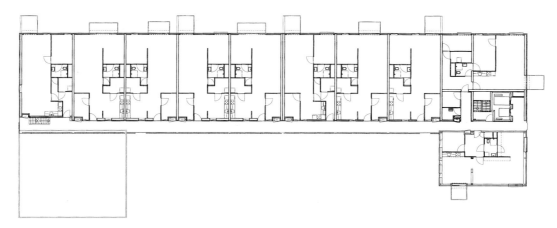

Seventh floor plan

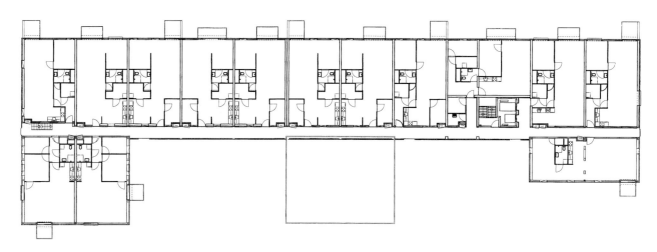

Sixth floor plan

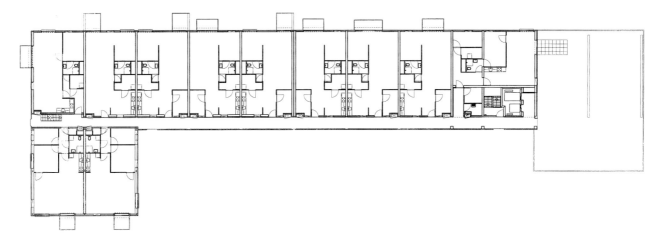

Fifth floor plan

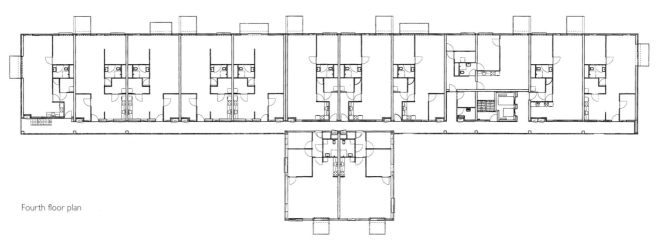

Fourth floor plan

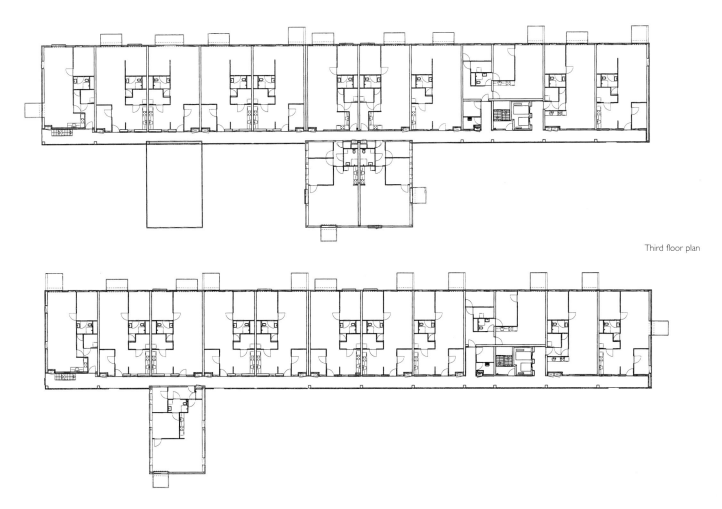

Third floor plan

Second floor plan

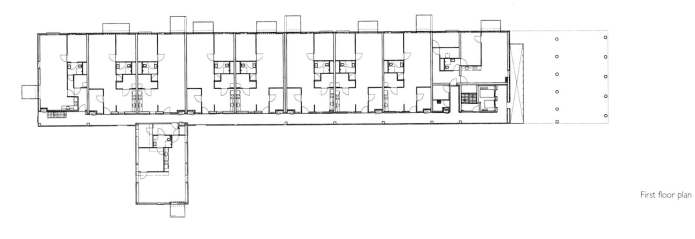

First floor plan

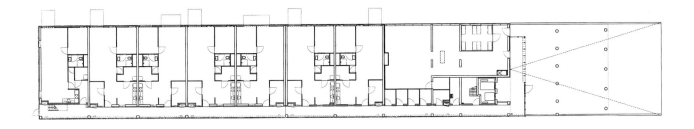

Ground floor plan

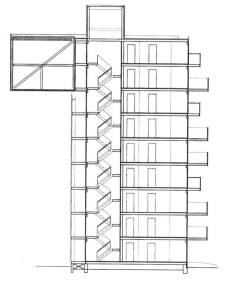

Cross sections

A great wealth and variety of forms and materials was necessary in the design of the openings in order to provide the individuality required by each apartment.

Thirteen of the one hundred apartments are completely suspended from the north facade by means of a system of triangular metal beams that absorb the large overhang.

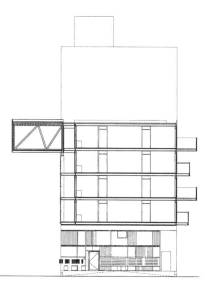

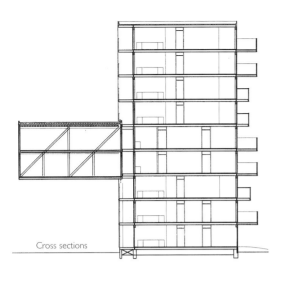
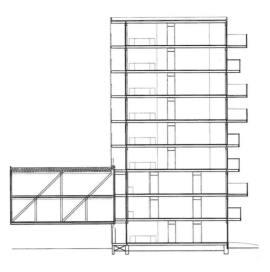

Cross sections

Toyo Ito
Housing for the elderly

Yatsuhiro, Japan

Nursing homes typically adhere to the organisational model of the hospital because it allows for an efficient administration, but this tends to produce an architecture of confinement that Toyo Ito tried to avoid in this project.

The building is sited in new reclaimed land by a hot spring resort town with views of the Amakusa Islands across the sea. The site's popularity among the townspeople, the local community's desire that the facility contribute new energy to the old town, and the facility's intent to offer its residents an environment for active, socially engaged lives, encouraged Ito towards a freer, more ambiguous configuration of space in a traditionally "closed" building type.

The flat roof is punctured by oval holes of contrasting size. It employs metal roof decking with a 100 mm-high flange, the structure of which was treated as a continuous series of shallow secondary beams. As such, only primary beams were necessary across the breadth of the roof, and these beams were hidden within the joints between the decking panels so as to emphasise the flat, lightweight form of the roof.

Supporting the flat roof are free-standing, two-level high reinforced concrete walls, placed in irregular locations, and columns of steel pipe. Since the free-standing walls receive the building's entire horizontal force – with only lateral force going to the steel pipes – columns of extremely slender proportion were sufficient. In contrast to the systematised structure of the roof, the elements below – whether colour, materials, or places – are distributed without interrelationship, so as to be marked almost by a sense of fracture. Light and rain enter through the holes in the roof, while the exterior scenery is drawn below the roof as a film-image-like scenery. The result: fictive "scenes", like dream fragments, suspended in highly transparent space, open and infused with natural light.

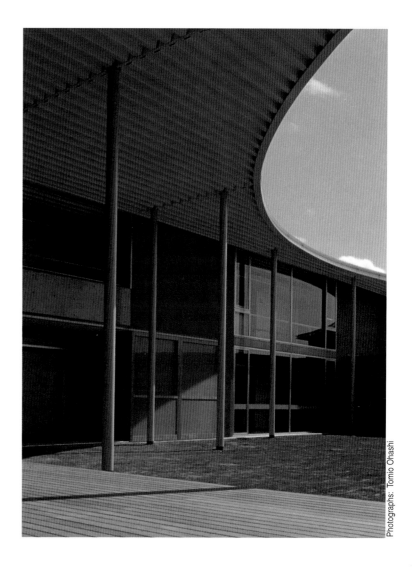

Photographs: Tomio Ohashi

50

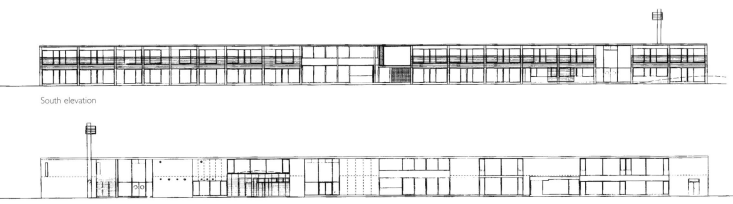

South elevation

North elevation

Site plan

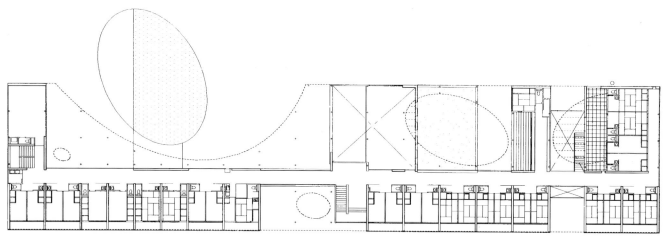

First floor plan

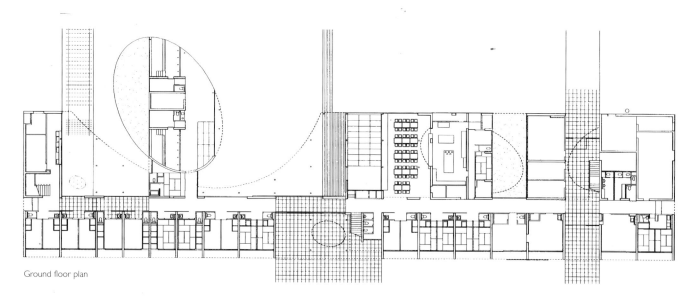

Ground floor plan

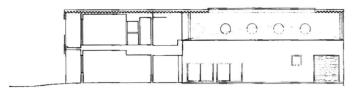

Cross section

East elevation

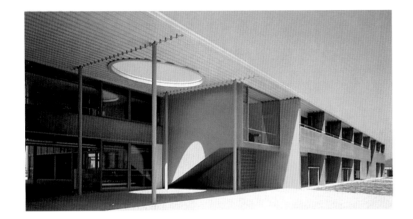

The roof, supported by reinforced concrete walls and thin hollow metal pillars, was perforated in places by oval holes of different sizes. Its extreme flatness and lightness is only interrupted by a 100 mm trim around the perimeter. Functionally, the project is organised as small open fragments distributed under the same roof, which gives unity to the spaces.

Klaus Kada

Geriatric home

Leibnitz, Austria

This small nursing home with 19 single rooms is composed of two separate elements set 2 degrees out of the parallel to each other. The approximately square building contains the administration, kitchen, communal area and the entrance to the living section on the ground floor. On the upper floor there are different treatment facilities and private rooms with balconies. The visitor's entrance is clearly characterised by a suspended canopy that protrudes far from the wall; the entrance for staff and suppliers is situated at the side towards the rear. The porch and the administration and sanitary rooms form the northern end of the building, facing the forecourt. A multi-functional lounge occupying most of the ground floor opens to the south and is only bounded to the west by the kitchen. The ground floor is structured by the top-lit main staircase standing next to the lift.

The small chapel, which is open at the top, has a red wall with timber cladding and is designed in the form of a parabola. This element consciously places an accent of colour in an otherwise very reserved space. Special attention was paid to the interior organisation and circulation. The treatment rooms and living units on the upper floor are reached by a gallery overlooking the ground floor. A short bridge leads to the common room, which has full-height glazing. The rooms have generous balconies (or terraces on the ground floor) that are protected against the western sun by the overhanging roof. The east entrance to the individual rooms is a cantilevered walkway with steps at the ends.

The construction system consists of reinforced concrete pillars and plates to avoid girders and beams and provide flexibility and the impression of lightness.

This impression is further emphasised by the glass and timber cladding and by the high window that makes the slightly inward-sloping roof appear to float.

Photographs: Angelo Kaunat

On the exterior, the large suspended canopy shows the visitors the access point to the building.

Roof plan

First floor plan

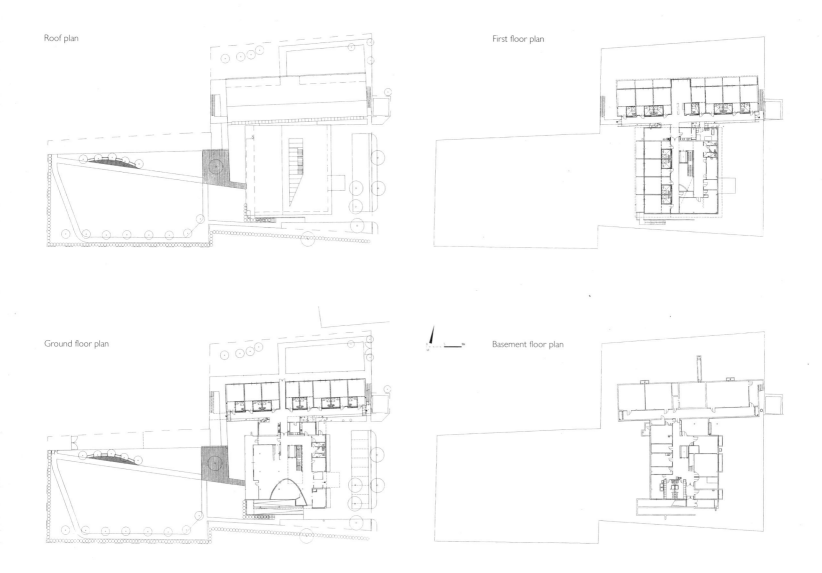

Ground floor plan

Basement floor plan

The two blocks, which are clearly distinct from the point of view of their construction, are articulated by means of a totally glazed gallery.

The rooms on the upper floor are reached by a projecting walkway that also protects them from the strong sunlight.

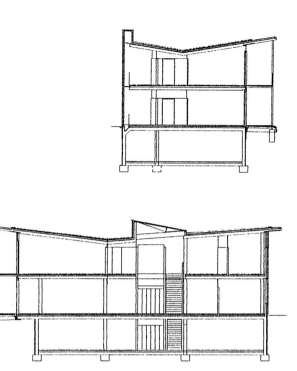

Cross sections

The small chapel, defined by a curved red wall, receives natural light through an opening in the roof.

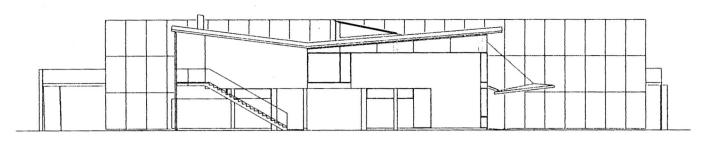

East elevation

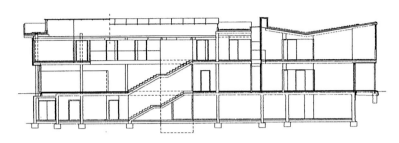

Longitudinal section

Soisick Cleret

Maison pour personnes agées dependants

Vitry-sur-Seine, France

This project, designed by the architect Soisick Cleret, is built in the vicinity of the town of Vitry-sur-Seine. It has a simple distribution comprising several pavilions of double height, organised in a comb form around a common axis of circulation and collective facilities. From the exterior, the building is seen as a work of great plasticity, in which Cleret has skillfully, almost like a tailor, used the warmth and expressiveness that zinc and wood give to the external fabric of the pavilions. Against the orthogonal nature of the general layout of the ground plan, one element stands out in the axial volume of circulation: a stone wall that runs from the line of the west facade, pointing out the main access.

A large lobby area, which is transparent and very bright, is filled with natural light coming through glazed openings in the roof. This area is conceived as a place of encounter among the residents. It is furnished with seats, tables and armchairs, and is also the place from which two staircases lead the residents to the 72 rooms of the centre.

The programme has been designed so as to allow the senior citizens to enjoy a high degree of independence and intimacy in their bedrooms —all fitted with small kitchen— and to offer them splendid views of the garden and the surrounding rural landscape.

Photographs: Patrick Tourneboeuf

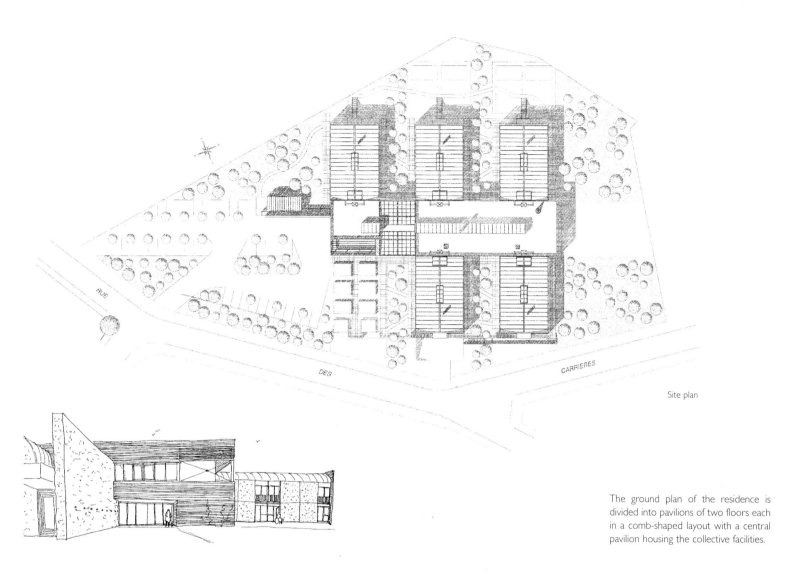

Site plan

The ground plan of the residence is divided into pavilions of two floors each in a comb-shaped layout with a central pavilion housing the collective facilities.

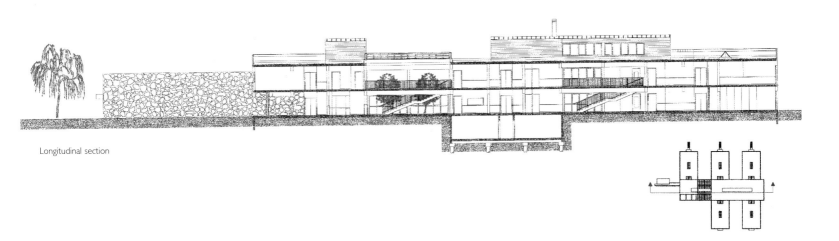

Longitudinal section

The access area located in the central part receives a great amount of natural light through glazed openings in the roof. The dwellings are accessed by two staircases that rise from this large space.

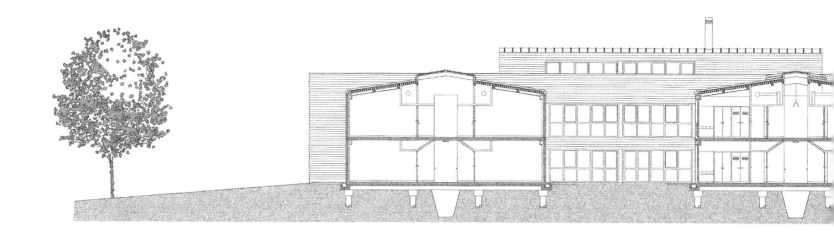

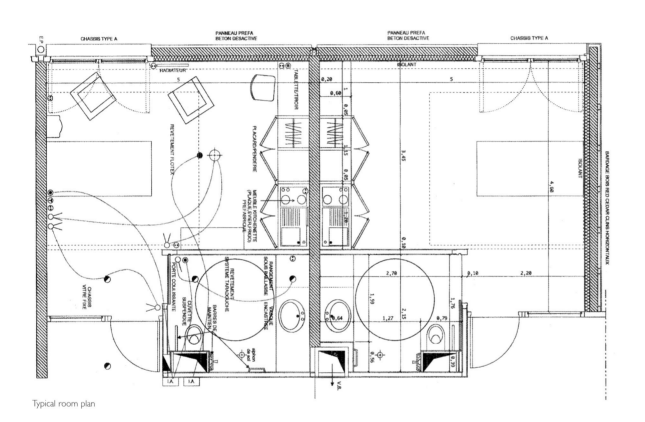

Typical room plan

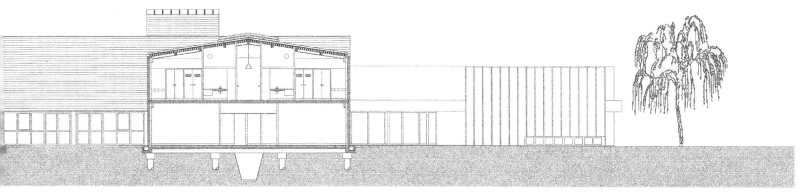

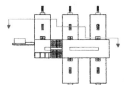

Longitudinal section trough the rooms

The structuring and organisation of the rooms facilitates the autonomy of the residents. All of them face the garden.

Thierry Nabères & Jacques Fourcade

Maison pour personnes agées

Montréal du Gers, France

The programme of a residence for the elderly requires the articulation of two dimensions: the independence of the elderly persons, with all the elements of their personal history, familiar objects and habits that this entails, and their insertion in a group that can provide a spatial and social environment suitable for situations of increasing dependence.

The architect Thierry Nabères, in association with Jacques Fourcade, has skilfully incorporated these opposing considerations into his design for 29 units of sheltered housing and attendant communal spaces (dining room, infirmary, sitting room, etc.).

The project, completed in 1995, executed within the framework of Plan et Construction's SEPIA programme (experimental, innovative housing for the elderly), had as its starting point an old country house on the banks of the Bastide. This was acquired by the municipality because of its proximity to medical services and leisure activities.

The new construction conjugates, rather than extends, the old house. The latter dictates the outline of the new building, inspires the U-shaped plan around a courtyard that is semi-open to the street, and prompts the tiled roofing, overhangs and loggias. Some rare architectural elements (the facade, a stone wall in a staircase) provide a tactile dimension within the plain universe of functionalism. The sloping land inspired the idea of diagonal screens that establishes the relationship of the house with its context.

Porches, stairs, ramps and galleries follow the slope of the land, and organise the house on 3 levels around an entrance courtyard and a more private garden. The 29 flatlets are grouped in clusters of 6 to 12 under an identifiable roof. An interior passageway links these clusters (balcony, loggia gallery) and forms a shared, fluid space that gives dignity to these hard elements of the programme.

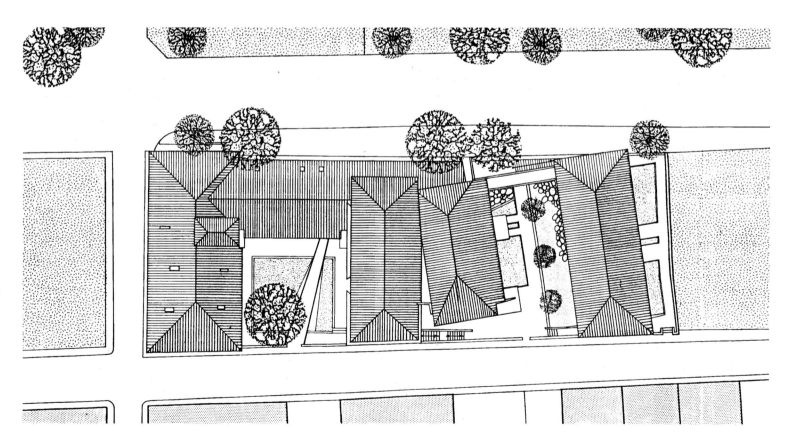

The new building conjugates and takes advantage of some of the formal aspects introduced by the existing building, reinterpreting certain elements such as the sloping tiled roof, overhanging cornices and balconies.

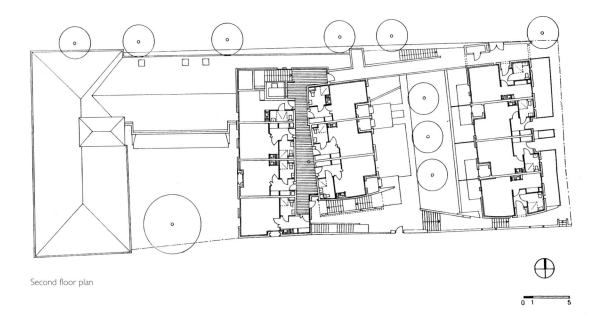

Second floor plan

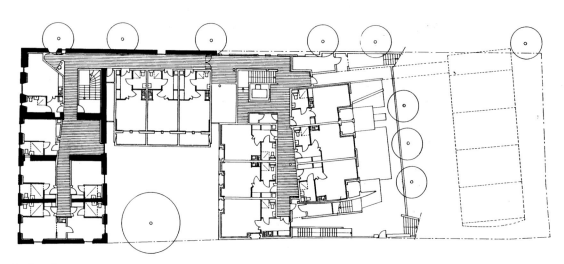

First floor plan

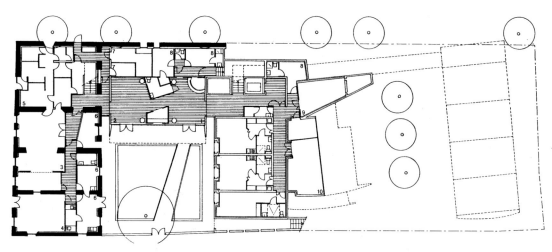

Ground floor plan

North elevation

South elevation

The location of the residence was chosen by the municipality due to its proximity to the medical and leisure facilities of the town.

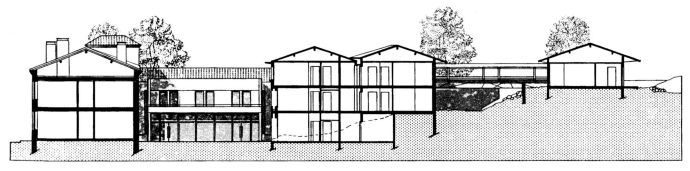

Longitudinal section

Cross-section

Repeating the layout of the existing building, the floor plan of the new building is organized in a U-shape around an inner courtyard that is partially open to the street. Most of the communal spaces are open onto the inner courtyard.

Magendie, Fauconnet & Leopold
Hospital de Maison Blanche
Neully -sur- Marne, France

The programme was to make an elderly residence with 120 beds by converting three buildings of a former psychiatry unit adjoining a hospital. In order to provide a suitable environment for elderly persons, the architects started from three ideas: to consider the residents as boarders rather than patients; to create a warm building and a medical institution capable of providing the necessary health care; and to provide a space that the boarders could make their own, offering privacy and contact, calm and activity.

Three of the pavilions were converted to offer each individual his/her own territory. The architects preferred to work within the present partitions, even if this led to oversized rooms. The former corridor was replaced with a transition space inviting movement between the common and private spaces. Each room is thus experienced as a house from which one can observe the movements of the other boarders and the staff. The central access space is treated as a public place and concentrates all the flows and movements generated by the institution: cars, visits, walks, group activities... It is a natural prolongation of the new building towards the south, creating a link and tension between the three pavilions.

The form of the new building is the direct result of the functional need to reduce the distance between the pavilions as far as possible, and is treated as an interior street. It is a light simple building for reasons of economy, with a masonry wall to the north and a glazed wall to the south. It is divided into communal spaces to the south and services to the north. The south facade can be extended onto a terrace to prolong the interior activities (summer dining area, etc.). At the two ends of the street are the hard and permanent areas, the technical facilities to the west, and the services linking with the logistic services of the hospital to the east.

Photographs: Vigneron

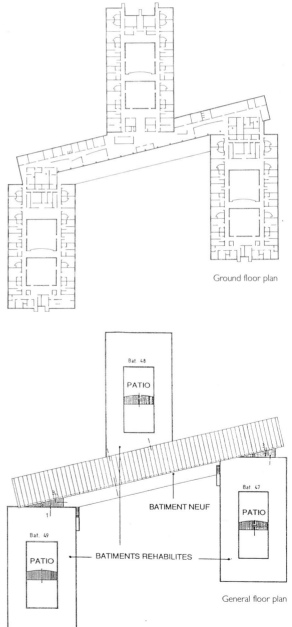

Ground floor plan

BATIMENT NEUF

BATIMENTS REHABILITES

General floor plan

Cross section

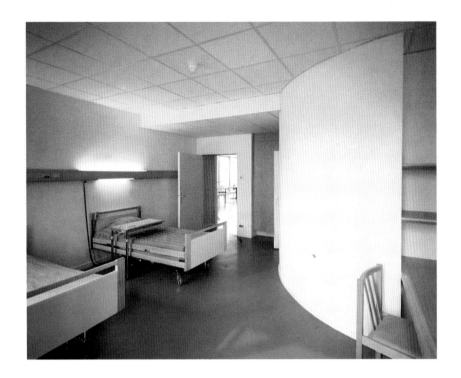

As can be seen below, a constant perception of the interior of the rooms is possible, whilst a high degree of privacy is maintained. The common spaces are extended towards the exterior by placing them against a south-facing glass wall.

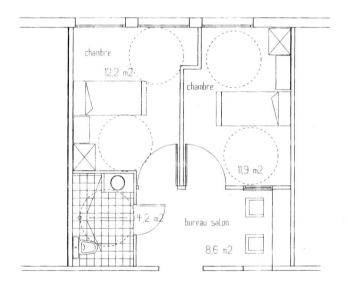

chambre
12,2 m2

chambre

11,9 m2

bureau salon

8,6 m2

4,2 m2

Plans of two different types of room

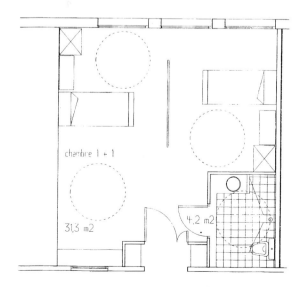

chambre 1 + 1

31,3 m2

4,2 m2

Arkkitehtitoimisto NVØ

Housing for Seniors

Kiuruvesi, Finland

Built on the banks of a lake, this Finnish residence has a privileged site which deserves to be taken advantage of in the design. The architectural language avoids imitation of the past, but turns decidedly towards the future in order to show that a residence of this type does not have to equal enclosure. Kiruvesi is a town dominated by a landscape of navigable cultures and paths. Situated near the cemetery, the retirement home is set in a slightly undulating meadow beside Lake Kiurujärvi, near the mouth of the river Kuorevirta with a bell tower in the background. There are thus many visual sequences that the architects have used to diversify the points of view proposed to the residents of the home. In order to avoid flooding, the building is situated at the highest point of the land. The surroundings of the lake are treated as a natural park. Less interesting is the presence of the motorway, which has led the architects to mix the profile of the construction with the vegetation. Elements such as the units for wastewater treatment determined the orientation of the building.

The winding building is organised around four functional units that are related to each other by a central column in the form of a fishbone. The independent apartments are situated near the town, as is the day centre, and between them are the services of the retirement home; at the end of the chain, the five units of rooms have been situated, each one for eight residents. A long central artery houses the common rooms and the circulation functions through an interior street with all the characteristics of an outdoor street: in each unit there are views of the surrounding landscape and chance encounters between the residents. The rejection of orthogonality due to the different levels of the volumes that intercept each other create unusual angles and oblique lines.

Photographs: Raimo Ahonen

The design clearly took advantage of a privileged setting near to a lake, avoiding the standard design of old people's homes. The home is at the mouth of the river Kuorevita, at the highest point of the outskirts of the town of Kiuruvesi, with a landscape of cultures and navigable routes.

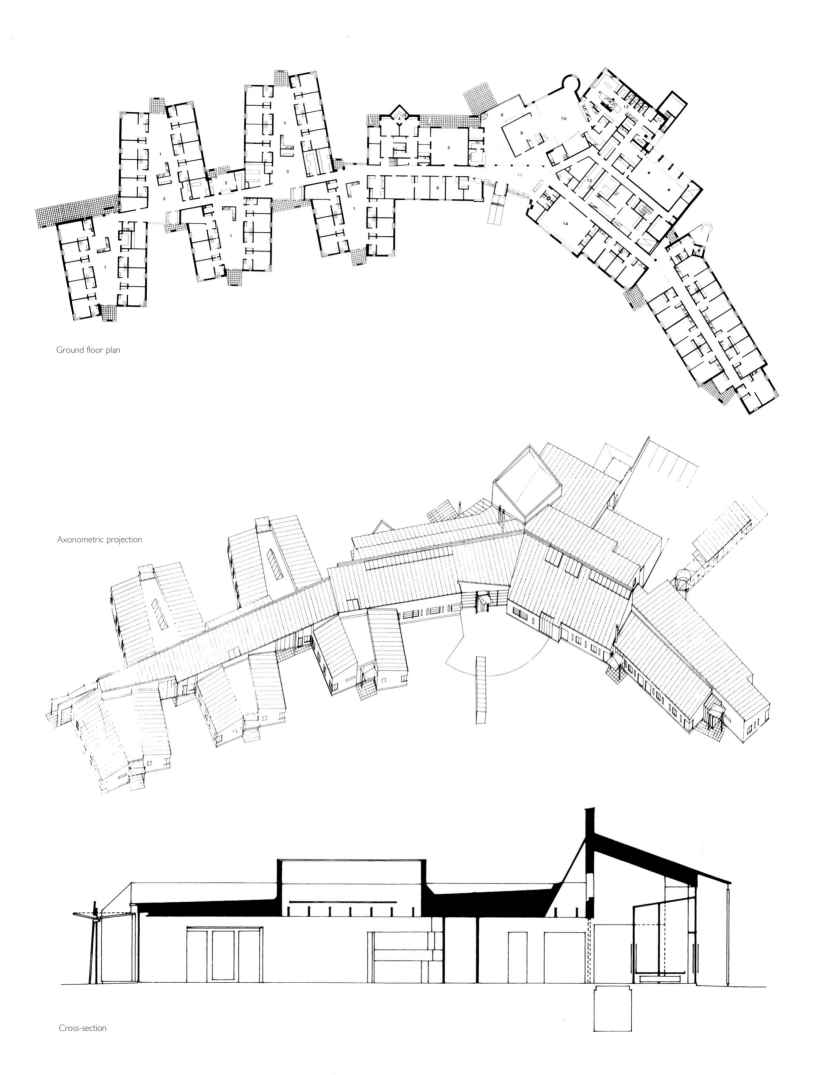

Ground floor plan

Axonometric projection

Cross-section

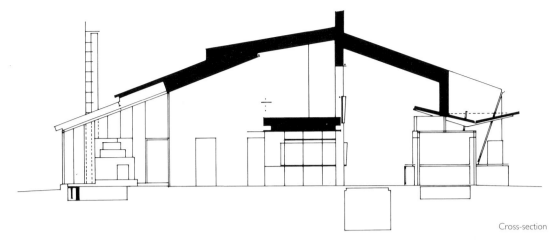

The construction was based on a functional, light and ethereal design, in which the conventional comforts were compensated for with the variety of finishes. Left: The building has a sinuous ground plan consisting of four functional units connected to each other by a corridor that operates as a central axis.

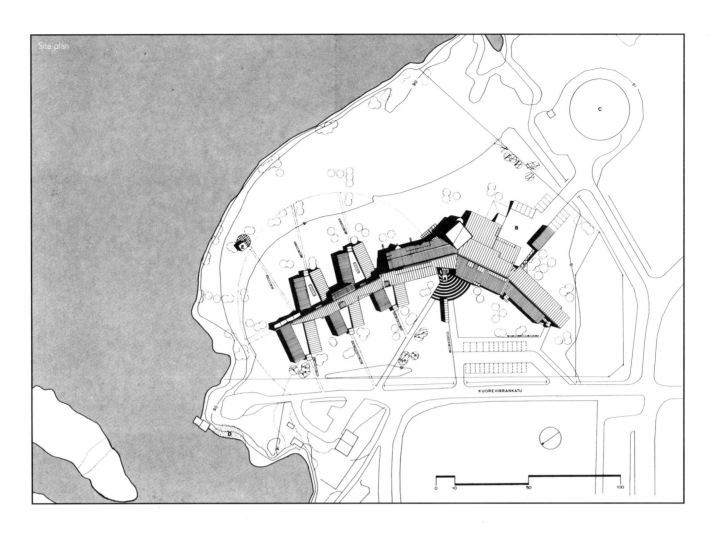

Site plan

Josep Lluís Mateo & Jaume Avellaneda

Residencia de Ancianos

Campdevànol, Spain

The landscape of Campdevànol is now characterised by the presence of abandoned factories in the middle of the valleys, and the population is marked by a large number of senior citizens, mostly people who once worked in the factories. This residence was built for them. The building is an elongated tablet placed parallel to the road that penetrates the valley. Set on a slope, it functions partly as a retaining wall and presents two highly differentiated longitudinal facades, the front facing the road and, blessed with sunshine and fine views, the rear looking north to the mountain. Like the facades, the floor plans respond to the topographic conditions, giving rise to a complex interplay of contrasts. Likewise, the east and west facades address similar principles: The east facade, the first to be discerned by the visitor coming in from town, reveals the thickness of the building, while the opposite end of the tablet, with its view of the landscape in all its splendor, serves to

open the building to the exterior by becoming a sort of ship's prow. The first floor of the building contains the general technical facilities and public access areas; care services are situated on the first floor; the private rooms and communal living rooms are organised on the second and third floor.

Both the structural systems and the interaction of materials seek to reinforce the articulation logic and the interplay of contrasts present in the composition of the facades. The south elevation reflects the different sizes of the rooms and combines the stone cladding of the larger panel with the zinc of the projecting pieces. This facade gives out a solid and grave image that is alleviated by the lightness and the movement of the road below. The north facade is built with blocks of concrete, a cheap material creating a special tension with the sophisticated technology that was used in the lintels in order to allow long horizontal openings.

Photographs: Duccio Malagamba

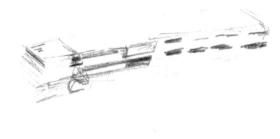

The building, a long tablet, has totally differentiated longitudinal facades: on the south side facing the road and on the north side facing the mountains.

The construction systems and the materials were used to reinforce the contrasts that appear in the composition of the facades.

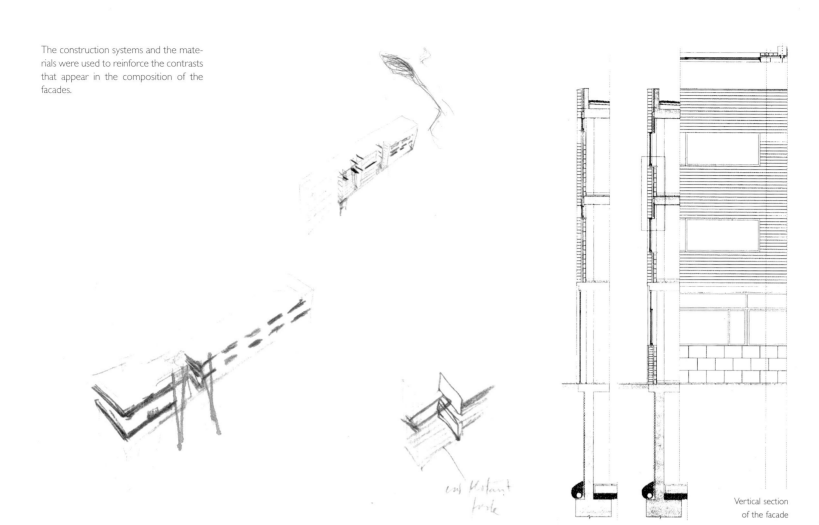

Vertical section
of the facade

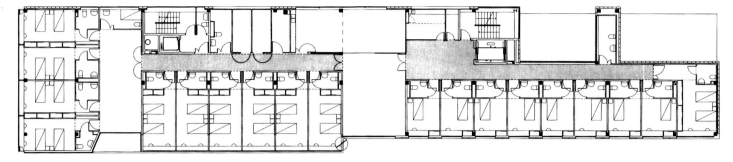

Upper level floor plan

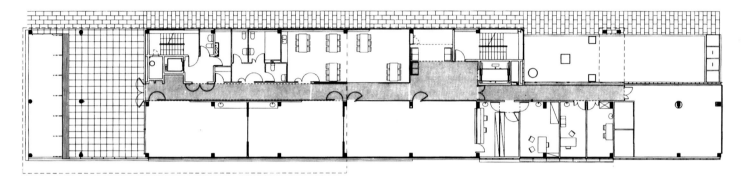

Ground floor plan

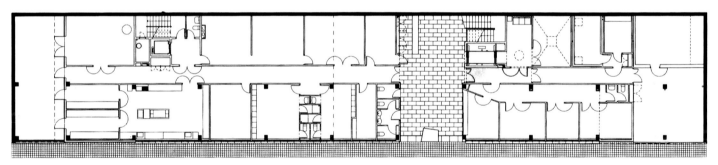

Basement plan

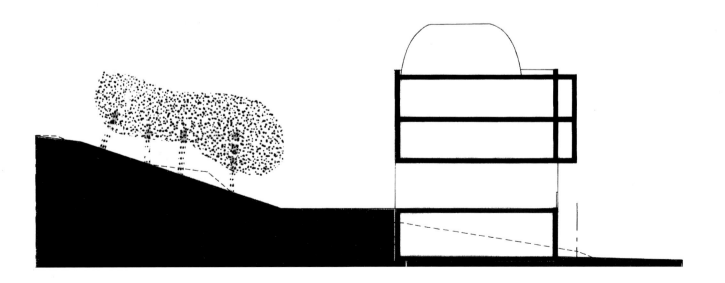

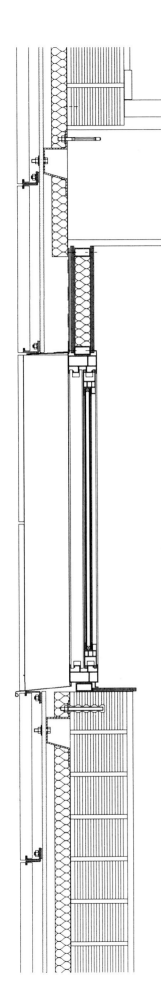
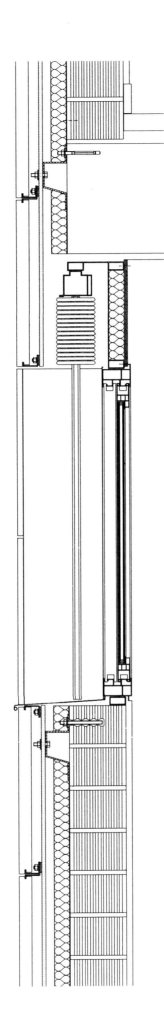
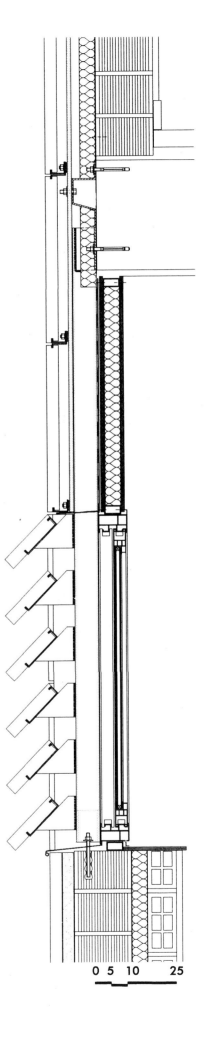

0 5 10 25

Details of the construction solutions on the facade

The building has four floors. The ground floor houses the access zones, the first floor the care services and the second and the third floors the bedrooms and common zones for relations between the residents.

The east-facing wall, with a wide outlook onto the surrounding landscape, transforms the end of the building into a sort of boat prow.

Wiel Arets

Two housing projects for the elderly

Tilburg & Maastricht, The Netherlands

Situated in a working class area dating from the 1930's, this is a complex of 20 apartments stacked into a four-storey building oriented towards the south-east in order to enjoy a large green public common. On this very public side there is a perforated aluminium screen with a mediating space behind. These galleries and the screen act as a filter between the public street and the private interior. The tenants inhabit this 3 m deep space which functions as a circulation, communication, and social arena that is visually connected to the surroundings through the perforated screen, although they are hidden from view from the outside. A brick facade with individual balconies faces north-west where the buildings' garden is designed as a collective outdoor space.

In the case of Tilburg, the two blocks are situated in a former industrial zone which is being transformed into a new cultural area combined with social housing projects. The social housing project is divided into two parts and the combined 67 apartments in both blocks are designed for elderly people. The two parts relate to the museum in quite different ways. One, a V-shaped block, positions itself up against the side of the museum to create an internal garden, the other, a longitudinal block, overlooks the museum garden.

Each apartment is 77 m² and has a living room, bedroom, kitchen and bathroom, considered to be the social standard for contemporary Dutch housing. The public facade of the blocks is in rough stucco or putz with internal balconies from which each apartment can overlook the road.

The private facade overlooking the garden is made of translucent glass brick with large openings. Behind this facade and between the individual apartment and the garden lies a 3 m corridor –an in-between space, a medium, a place to meet, but also to sit and relax.

Photographs: Kim Zwarts

Site plan

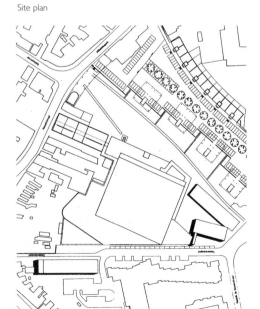

90

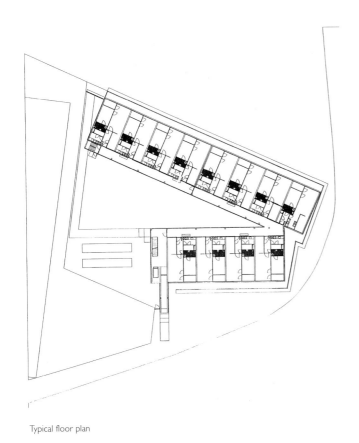

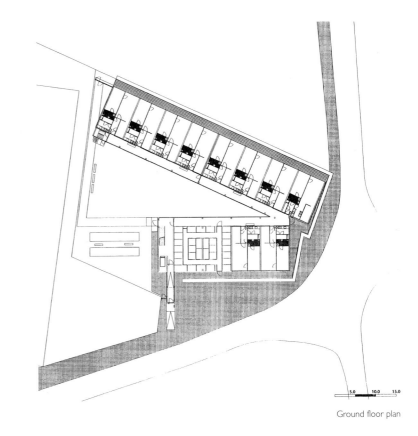

Typical floor plan

Ground floor plan

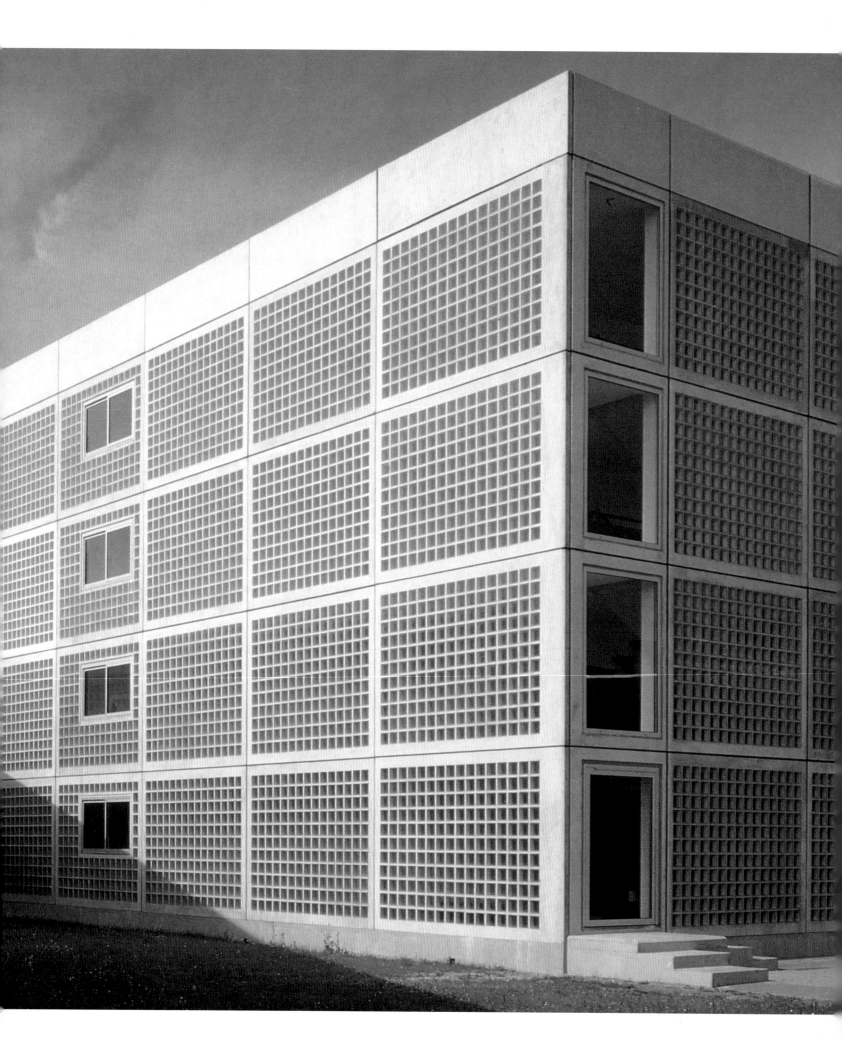

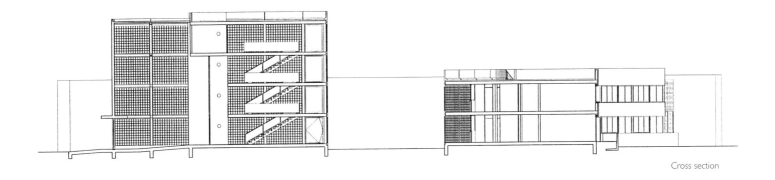

Cross section

The facades that look onto the inner courtyard, behind which are the access galleries to the dwellings, are entirely built of glass blocks.

The large surfaces of translucent glass, only interrupted by the structural framework of concrete, allow light into the access and distribution areas.

DWELLINGS FOR THE ELDERLY AT MAASTRICHT

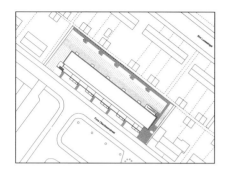

Site plan

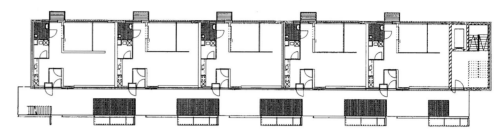

Typical floor plan

Ground floor plan

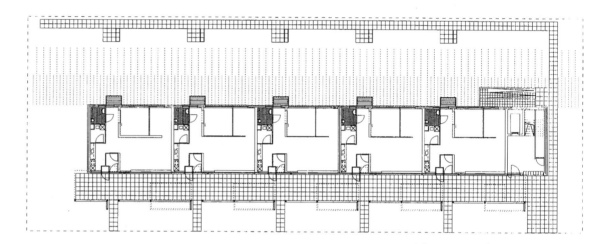

The dwellings are separated from the public space by a generous 3.2 metre-wide access gallery which functions as a circulation, communication and social area.

Detail of exterior staircase

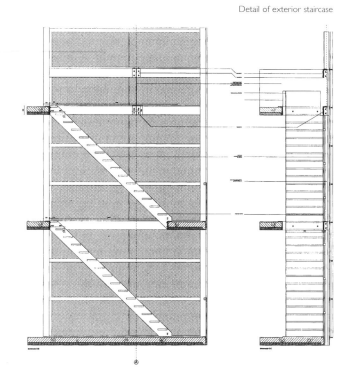

Toshio Akimoto

Yakult Dormitory

Tokyo, Japan

This project is the result of a contest put out by the Yacult Corporation for the design of small apartments for their employees.

The complex breaks down into eight volumes containing the small residential units, which rise from a concrete foundation and form a striking silhouette against the fragmented urban landscape of Hachioji in Tokyo.

The functional layout has been achieved with great simplicity. The apartments occupy the upper levels, contained within eight cubes of six metres a side, faced on the outside with a combination of pavisade and aluminium plate. And the general facilities -kitchen, laundry, office-, the manager's rooms and small bedrooms for guests are located on the ground floor, shared out between two buildings attached on the longer side of the rectangle. Between them a third free strip is partially occupied by a unit -also rectangular- which circles round to link the two buildings. The roof of

this unit, which is glass-walled on the ground level and houses a common sitting area and the entrance hall, is an area linking six of the eight residential modules to each other on the upper level and also provides access to them. Four apartments are located in each —two on each floor— all functioning as totally private houses thanks to their independent entrances.

Thus, the project has a two-fold nature. On the upper floor the unit has a domesticated air, noticeably different from conventional community residential architecture. And on the lower floor one sees an area dominated by the corner of the hall which receives visitors and the view of the small bridge which leads off to the apartments situated at the north-west end, evoking in some way the complexity of the traditional urban environment.

Photographs: Eiji Yonekura

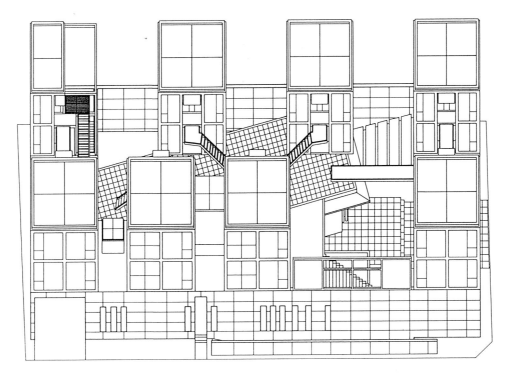

Axonometric view

The project is structured simply by means of eight six-metre cubes that were placed on the site. Each cube, built with aluminium, glass brick, blocks and reinforced concrete walls, houses four residential units. To the left, an aerial view of the complex from the north-west side.

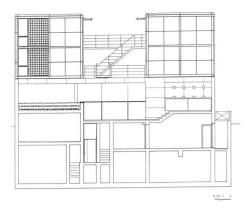

The ground floor was conceived as a space with an urban character. It houses the general facilities such as the kitchen, laundry, a small guest room and other community rooms.

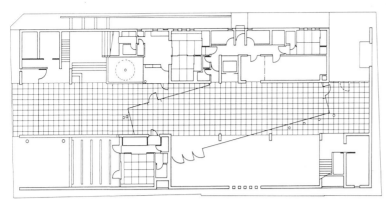

First floor plan

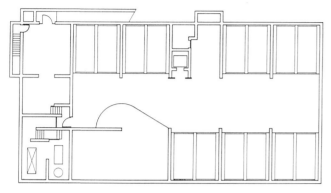

Basement floor plan

Each of the residential units has a direct access from the exterior and is thus independent. They are all joined by a common inner courtyard located on the second floor.

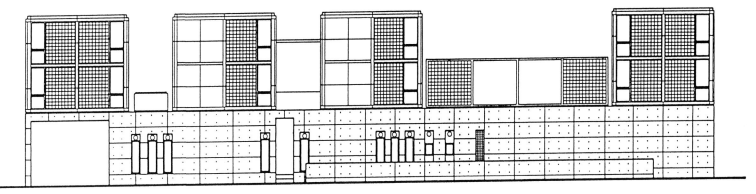

North elevation

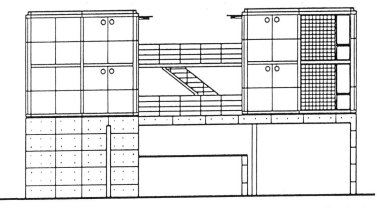

East elevation

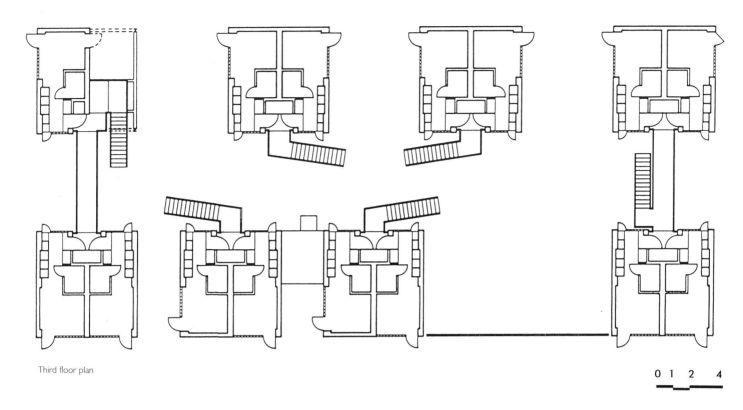

Third floor plan

0 1 2 4

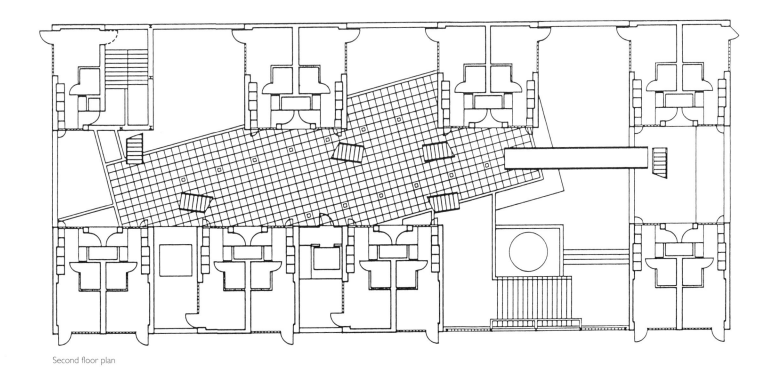

Second floor plan

Massimiliano Fuksas
Residence Universitaire Ville d'Herouville
Saint-Clair, France

The design idea that gave rise to the spatial structure is "building around voids". In relation to the existing fabric characterised by its great fragmentation, this project proposes to use the operation as a goal to bring together the whole. For this reason the building has been conceived as a single linearly developed element.

The project as a whole delimits and protects the south part of the Residence Universitaire and places it in contact with the city centre. Bearing in mind the requirements of the brief, and foreseeing a high number of parking spaces, a raised building was designed in which the car park is not concealed as it usually is, but becomes a positive element that participates in the life of the project. The project, on the Avenue de la Grande Cavée and the Boulevard de la Haute Folie, is clearly identifiable as it rises above the green spaces and the car park. The volumetric rupture, which is accentuated by the lack of urban continuity, is thus attenuated. Two parallel platforms contain the university residence block. On the side housing the rooms, the volume is sculpted by vertical zigzag plants, creating strong effects of light and shade. On the opposite side, where the circulation zone is located, the building shows an impeccable vertical rise and is broken down into planes of different colours. Through these perforations, through which the light enters depending on the position of the sun, it is possible to perceive the surprising exterior perspectives. In the wide low volume of the building, two large voids allow the natural light to enter the distribution zone and the interior of the rooms.

The east part, where the road goes under the building beside the open court, has a dynamic personality. The common facilities block is the element that fixes the building to the ground on piles, and is therefore a very readable element that fits into the geography. The bright colours of this suspended sculpture become an identifying symbol of this city.

Photographs: Philippe Ruait

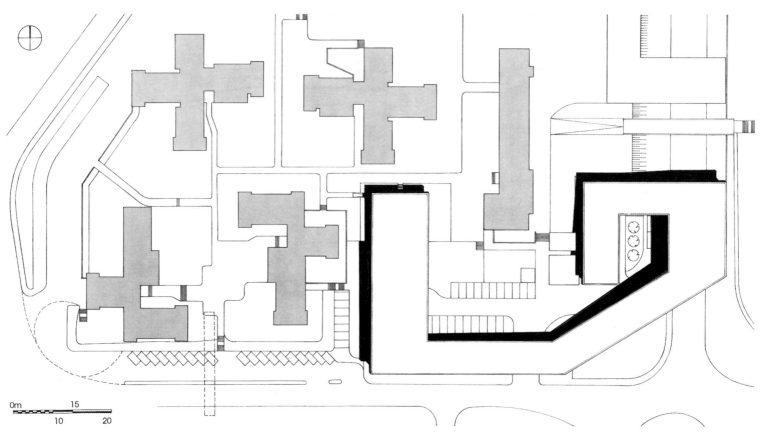

0m   15
  10   20

The building has been designed as a single element developed linearly. Adapting to a fragmented terrain, it was based on the concept of construction around voids.

South elevation

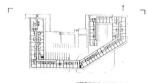

FACADE NORD   HEROUVILLE SAINT-CLAIR
RESIDENCE UNIVERSITAIRE

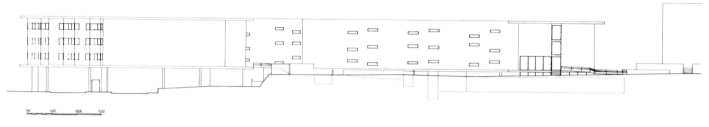

North elevation

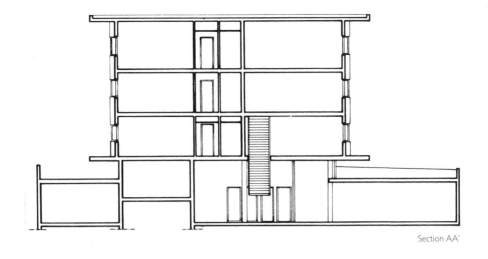

Section AA'

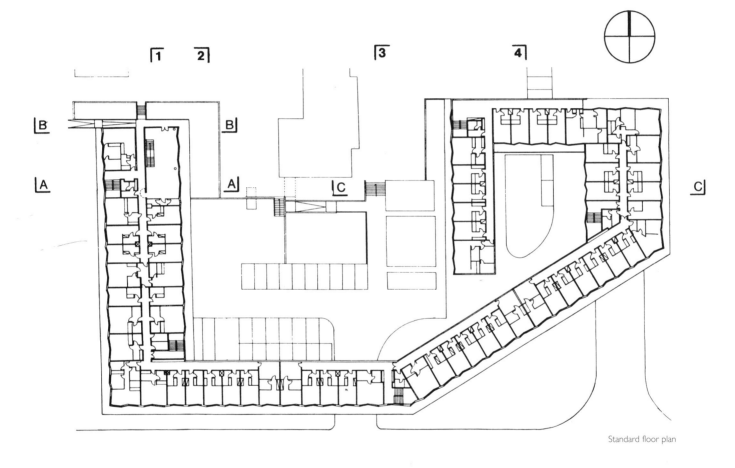

Standard floor plan

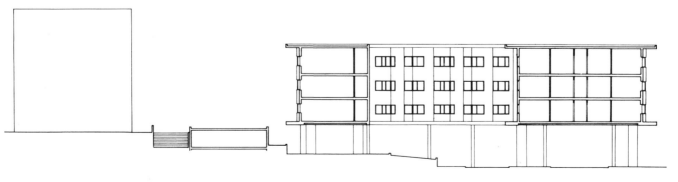

Section CC''

On one side, where the zone for motor vehicle transit is located, the building is decomposed impeccably into several vertical planes of different colours in zigzag. As a large number of parking spaces was required, the large parking space is not concealed, but becomes a positive element in the life of the project. With its different colours, it evolves and changes in time, both during the day and at night.

Left: The common service volume is an element that fits perfectly into the setting. Furthermore, the chromatic intensity of this "suspended sculpture" turns it into an authentic urban symbol.

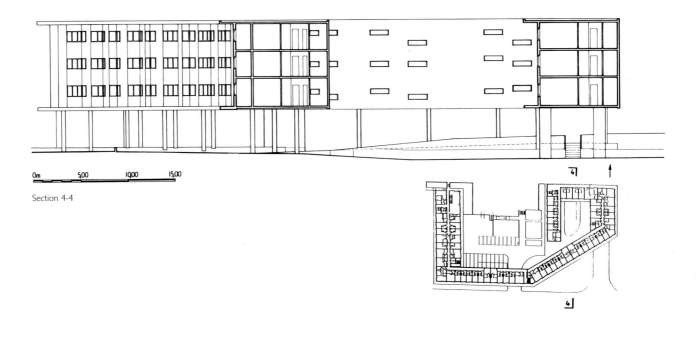

Section 4-4

0m 5,00 10,00 15,00

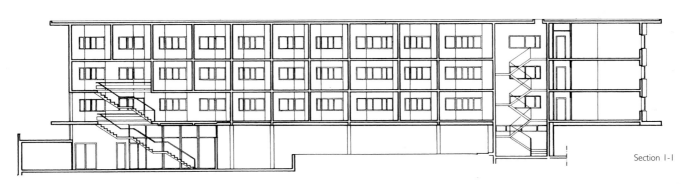

Section 1-1

Architecture Studio

University Residence

Paris, France

Framing what one wishes to see, shielding from what one does not want to suffer, inverting the bad into good, altering the negative constraints of the site to create a positive reality: that was the challenge facing this 351-student housing project built right on the edge of the peripheral zone of Porte de Clignancourt.

On the roadside there is a protective wall, a curved shield 30 by 100 metres, a giant screen, an enigmatic signal built into the kinetic landscape of the city as seen from the car.

The shield is a double space, inserted between two walls that are structured by red steel ties and through which three glazed lifts evolve. It is a Parisian promenade looking out towards the moving cars. The protecting wall is pierced at its centre by a large window that frames the suburban horizon towards the Saint-Denis basilica.

At night, this black concrete wall reflects the hues of the multi-coloured advertising neons and car headlights. The plate glass allows the building's interior light to filter outwards. Red beacons punctuate the isolated mass of this shield-rock.

On the Paris side, a green belt, tranquility, sun. Backing onto the shield, three curved buildings faced in aluminium. All the apartments are well sheltered within these three prows. The interior routes are set off by various spaces differing from the monumental entrance hall and the shield in order to give privacy to the apartments. The access to the latter is by double height landings. These are cut through by several plaster columns inset at intervals with round glass bricks, wells of natural light brought down to each landing from the roof. These light wells are a fixed point common to every floor. They look towards the sky from the heart of the building.

Thanks to the almond-shaped plan and splayed bay windows, every apartment is south-facing, with views towards the adjacent university gardens and the silhouette of Montmartre and the Sacré-Coeur.

Photographs: Patrick Tourneboeuf

The university residence building rises audaciously in a clearly urban setting surrounded by traffic and noise on one side and by a green belt of peace on the other.

0   10   20

East elevation

0   10   20

South elevation

113

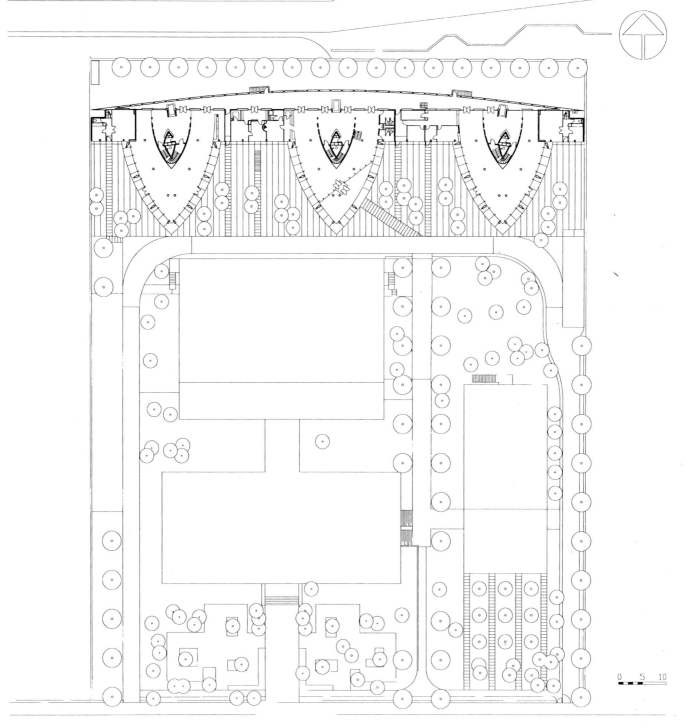

Ground floor plan

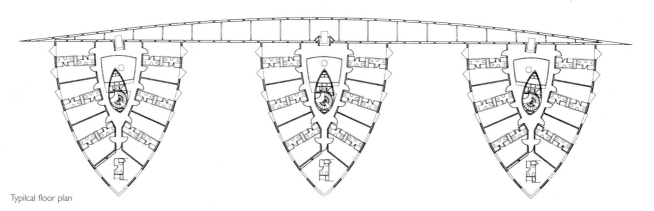

Typilcal floor plan

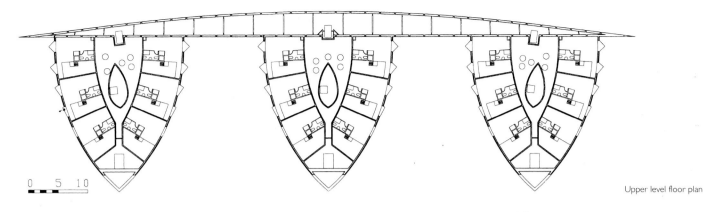

The protective wall has in the middle a large picture window that frames the suburban landscape of Saint Denis church. In order to provide as much privacy as possible in a setting with a great volume of traffic, an enormous protective shield, a 30x100-metre screen, was built.
The slanting glass of the outer walls allows the light generated from the inside of the building to be diffused to the exterior. The red lights interrupt and give rhythm to the monotonous grey stone wall.

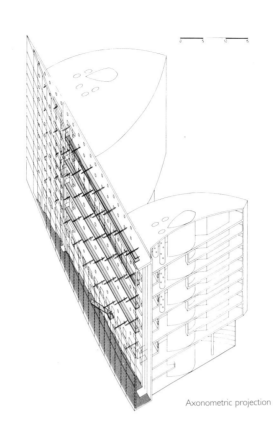

The access to some of the apartments is made through a double height landing. The interior routes are punctuated with plastered columns, glass blocks and points of natural light.

In order to preserve privacy, the interior routes of the buildings are further cut by different spaces, in contrast with the exterior homogeneity.

Axonometric projection

117

V.P. Tuominen Architects

Housing Complex

Helsinki, Finland

In 1991 the Housing Production Office (ATT) of the city of Helsinki, by order of Kiinteistö-HYKS Yo, arranged a 2-stage architectural competition for a house containing staff residences and to be built in Ruoholahti.

The competition aimed at finding a form of residential building which could be built as an ARABA production, taking into account as well as possible both the demands of comfortable living conditions and those made by the important location in the urban scenery.

The building site was located at a meeting between city blocks containing new residential houses and a large old industrial area beside the busy Porkkalankatu street and at the end of Itämerenkatu street.

The role of the house front as a background for Martii Aiha's Rumba sculpture made its own demands. These starting-points gave birth to a mass divided sharply into two parts: a side-passage house turning its glass back to the traffic.

The green reglit glass plank wall of the side passage forms a uniform background, but one which lives with the interior and exterior lighting. The chosen material is intended to harmonise with the surrounding industrial buildings. The light side passage also protects the dwellings of shift-working hospital staff from traffic noise and pollution. Most apartments are small two-room ones (2 rooms + kitchenette, 44.5 sqm), the bigger apartments being located at the ends of the building. The sauna department on the top floor opens onto the sea over Kaapelipuisto park.

Photographs: Jussi Tianen

The apartment block had to satisfy two priorities: to solve the demand for housing and to adapt to a difficult location in a complex urban setting.
A large greenish glass wall operates as an excellent neutral background for the sculpture "Rumba" by Marti Aiha that is placed in the square in front of the building.

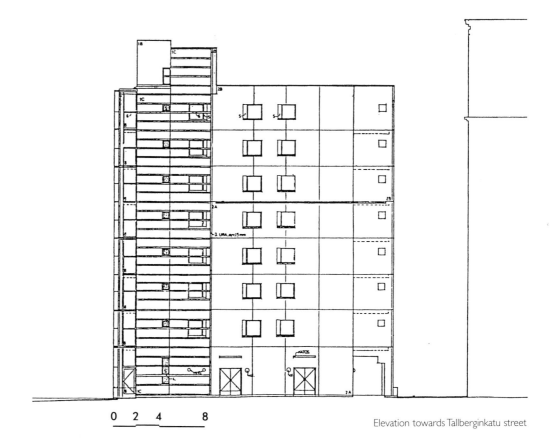

0 2 4   8

Elevation towards Tallberginkatu street

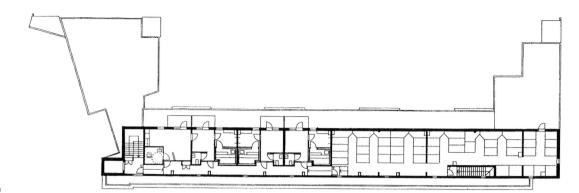

Eighth floor plan

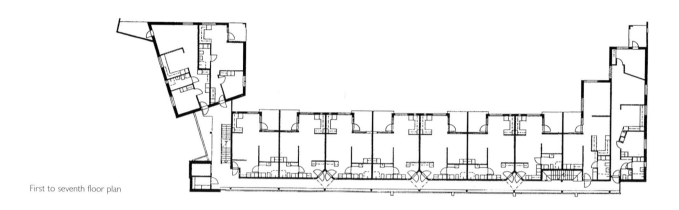

First to seventh floor plan

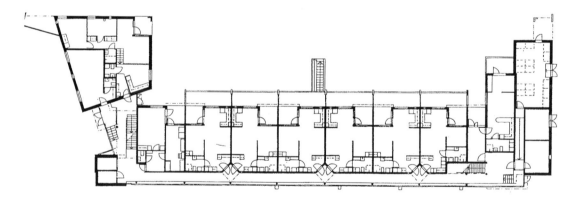

Ground floor plan

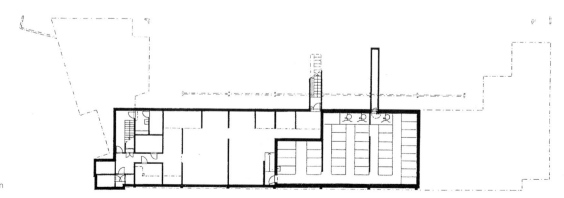

Basement floor plan

The building, situated between large residential blocks and a large industrial zone, emerges as a large constructed mass that is divided into two clearly differentiated parts by a large access corridor that turns its back on the traffic. The materials chosen seek harmony with the buildings of the industrial environment.

Several views of the corridor and staircase that provide access to the dwellings. On the side of these a void is created from which the succession of floors can be seen, as is shown in the photograph below.

The glass corridor that provides access to the dwellings also operates as a barrier against the noise of traffic and pollution outside.

Most of the apartments have a floor space of only 44.5 square metres, with the exception of those situated at the ends of the block.

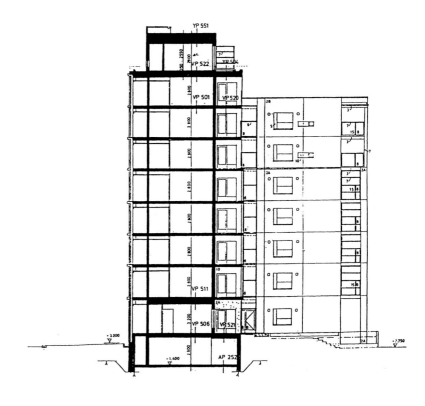

Cross section

Most apartments are small two-room ones (2 rooms + kitchenette), while the bigger apartments are located at the ends of the building. The sauna department on the top floor opens onto the sea over Kaa-pelipuisto park.

Francis Soler

Rue Emilie Durkheim

Paris, France

In this apartment building the idea of a totally flexible project in time served as guideline for the choice of the structural concept. A discontinued concrete "curtain" stretches across the longitudinal axis of the building. It is occasionally doubled to form vertical shafts such as staircases and elevators, which serve as bracing for structural stability. 73 columns, placed according to an irregular grid around the circumference of the floor plates, leave great liberty concerning the floor plan and the distribution of all the inner portions.

In the design of the facade, the idea was to provide floor-to-ceiling glazing in each apartment, with sliding frames to avoid space loss. The outer frames are made of black lacquered aluminium, and the inner frames are made of wood. The coloured, enamelled images are printed on the exterior glass facade. The narrow floor bands of the balconies are fixed to the circumference of the floor plates. There is no continuity of material to avoid thermal bridges.

In winter, cold outside air enters beneath the lower part of the outer aluminium frame, heats up in the intermediate glazed space and flows into the apartments through inlets in the upper part of the inner wooden frame. This effect has been taken into account for calculations. The double facade and this type of air circulation also provide a noise reduction.

The Jatoba wood boards of the balconies are an extension of the coloured resin floor inside. As a consequence of the structural principle all the inner partition walls are made of Placopan or Placostil, allowing flexibility for later changes. The walls and the ceilings are coated and painted white. Articulated metacrylate panels separate the kitchen space from the living area. In the bathroom red plastified wood boards with aluminium frames were preferred to the traditional tiles.

Photographs: Nicolas Borel

The motifs used to cover the glass facade are scenes taken from the frescos by Roman Giulio on the walls of the Palazzo del Té in Mantua. The use of colours that are as bright as the originals creates a clearly defined succession of mural images.

The brightness of the colours is enhanced under the influence of the light both by day and at night. The overlapping of different layers of images and texts gives the facade a dynamic and complex appearance.

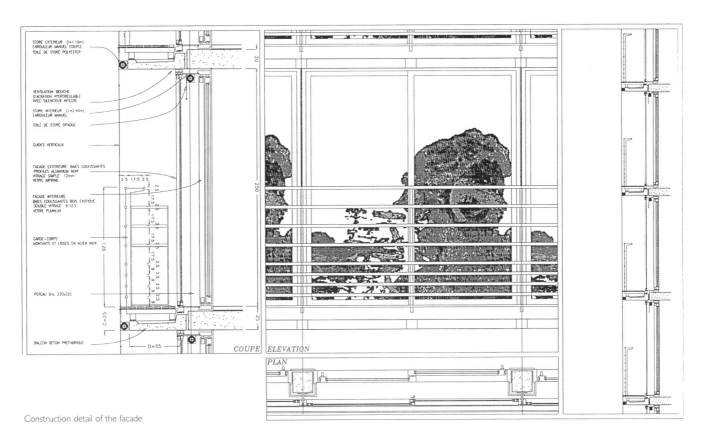

Construction detail of the facade

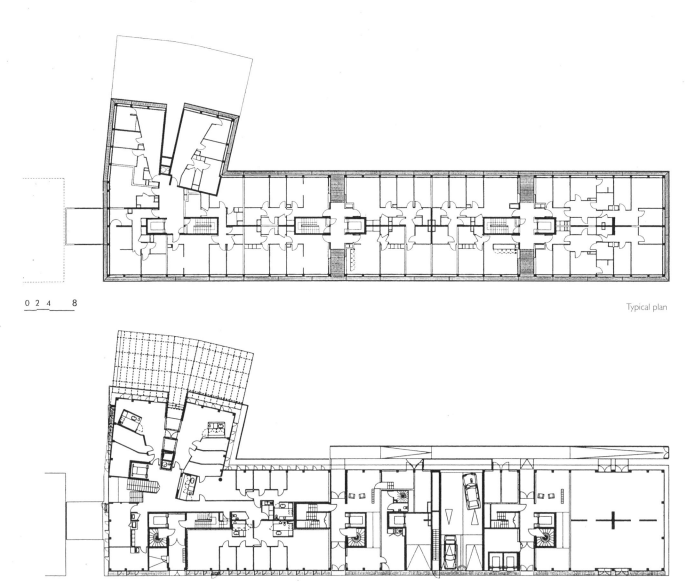

0 2 4 8

Typical plan

Ground floor plan

The wood used in the frames coexists in perfect harmony with the coloured resins of the pavements. The metal handrails of the facade provide rythm and a degree of geometrisation.

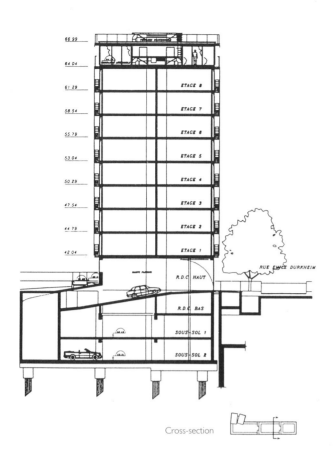

Cross-section

The accumulation of frescos allows the incoming natural light to be filtered, creating an appropiate atmosphere af intimacy in the interior spaces without the need for other types of filters.

Carlos Ferrater

Viviendas en la Calle Foix

Barcelona, Spain

This project consists of the construction of a multipurpose building located on the boundary between two uptown districts of Barcelona. Between the district of Sarrià and the valley of Trinquet, a fragmented strip edged with low interlocking residential buildings, a housing scheme is taking shape within the urban fabric of narrow streets. On the southeastern side a row of houses run parallel to the avenue below, forming a group of buildings linked longitudinally. Full advantage is taken of the slope of the street and regulations governing maximum construction height to create a series of stepped terrace on which the building's various facilities are housed. Due to the high location of the scheme, these terraces are in effect belvederes with magnificent views over the city.

The facade is clad in travertine, and adapts to both the slope of the land and the curve of the street. It produces a sober, luminous, ordered image, thanks to the continuity of design of each of the modules making up the scheme.

In the interior of the project, articulating its cross-sections, the garage and the communal area are laid out following the internal corridors. These are lit by means of a series of courtyards, an open sunken walkway and a number of gaps in the roof. A succession of walkways and landscaped squares cover the level above.

The whole project can be regarded as an exercise in perfect integration into the urban and social framework in which it is set, following the habitual themes and plastic language of Carles Ferrater's work.

Photographs: Lluís Casals

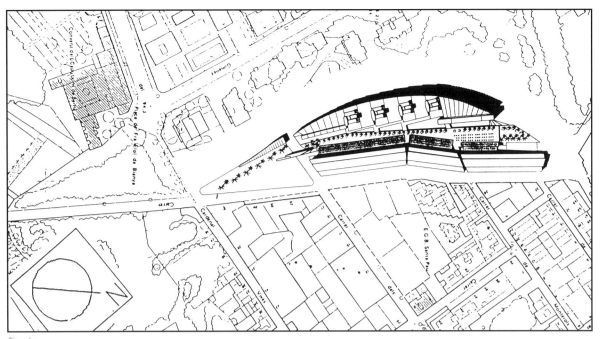

Site plan

The building is taller then those that surround it and therefore enjoys spectacular views of the mountain on one side and, on the other side, the neighbourhood of Sarrià.

The slope of the street has been used to create stepped terraces, which are open to excellent views of the city.

131

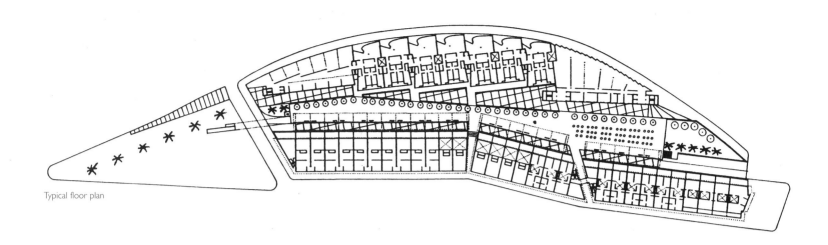

Typical floor plan

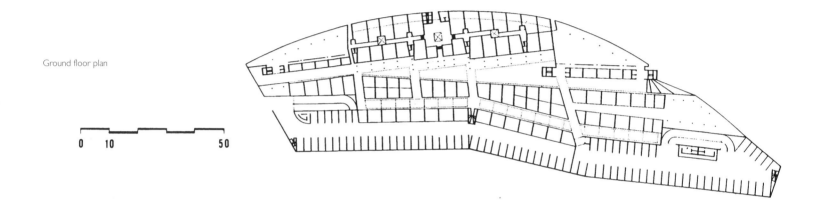

Ground floor plan

0   10   50

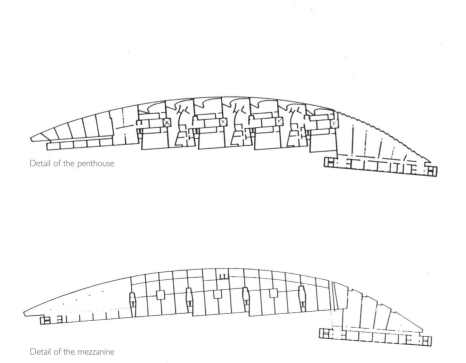

Detail of the penthouse

Detail of the mezzanine

The slope and curve of the street have been used to achieve a more plastic image. The terraces and windows of the building are arranged in a succession, creating a tidy and luminous atmosphere.

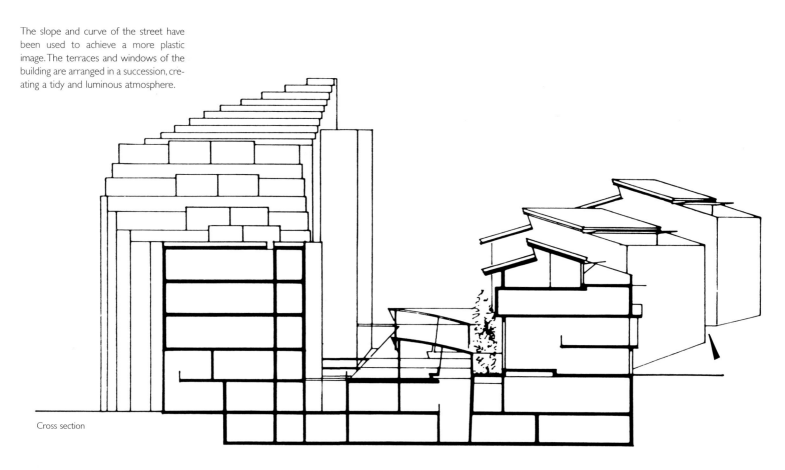

Cross section

Christian Sumi & Marianne Burkhalter
R. Albertin (Collaborator)

Apartment building in Laufenburg

Laufenburg, Switzerland

The project forms part of a general restructuring of the garden area of the old convent of Laufenburg that also includes a business school. The residential building and the school are linked to the existing buildings that determine the site. The business school is situated opposite the state school, a monumental building typical of the 19th century. The housing block, with a ground floor parking lot, is placed parallel to the shopping mall.

The project is located according to a set of historic references of houses with galleries and the recent interpretations that they have given rise to, including the Siedlung Dammerstock by Gropius in Karlsruhe, the Spangen district by Brinkmann in Rotterdamm, in 1919-21, the Golden Lane Housing by Peter and Alison Smithson in 1951-52, and the Gallaratese district by Rossi Aldo in Milan, in 1970-73.

The traditional country house with balconies to the south constitutes another reference of the project.

It is the rural counterpart of the urban house with galleries and is also found in the Alps. These balconies not only play a role of opening, they serve for drying hay or tobacco, and therefore form a work space. This is the type of concept that has been imagined for Laufenburg.

The single apartments are placed along the walkway, thus enabling –or provoking– a certain social communication. The living space has views to the north of the castle hill with the medieval tower and the church, the two landmarks of Laufenburg. The building is held together and given unity by the use of colour on the facade: dark-grey cement-fibre panels, light-blue railings and red/yellow front walls on the gallery.

The overlaying of a more urbane with a more rural typology corresponds to the semi-urban town-planning situation outside the medieval city-centre.

Photographs: Heinrich Helfenstein

136

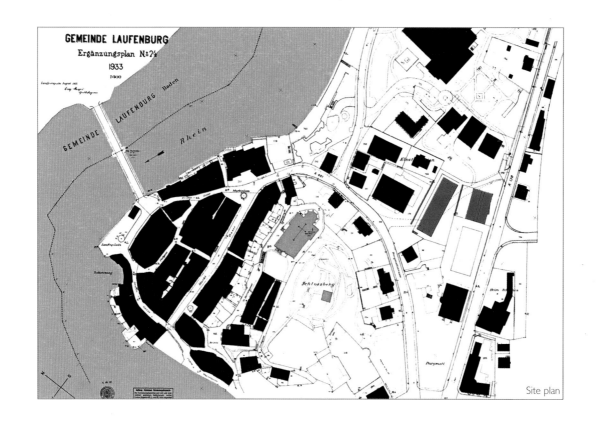

Site plan

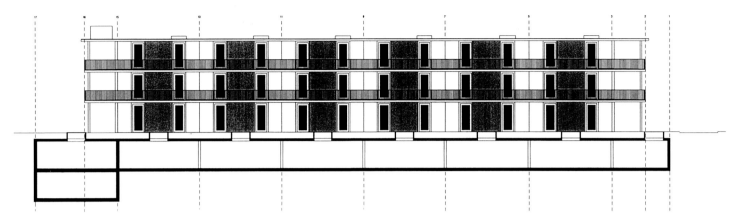

South elevation

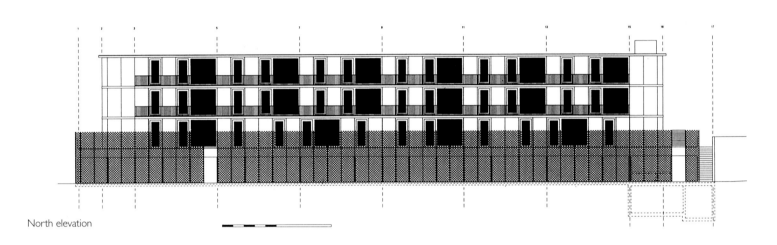

North elevation

Following the local tradition, the block is divided into wide external access galleries. Because of their width, these spaces become places of leisure and relations.

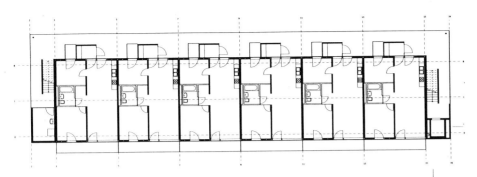

Typical floor plan

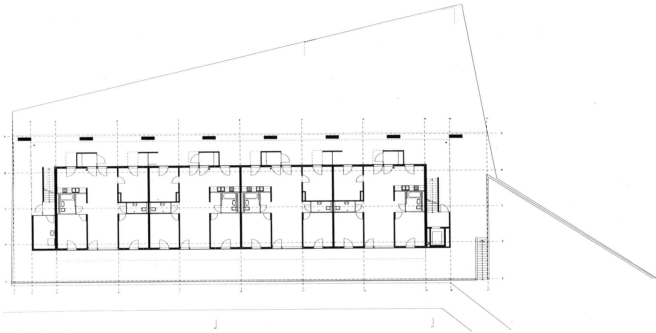

Ground floor plan

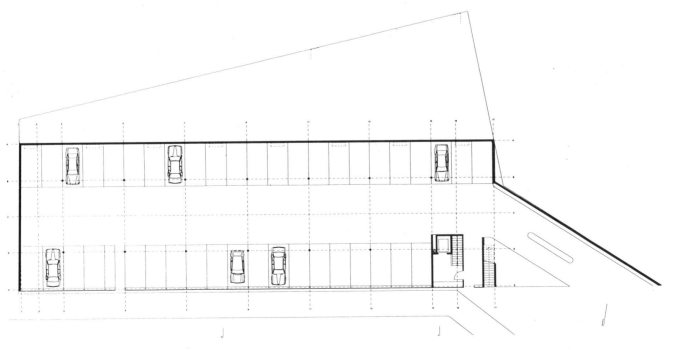

Garage floor

140

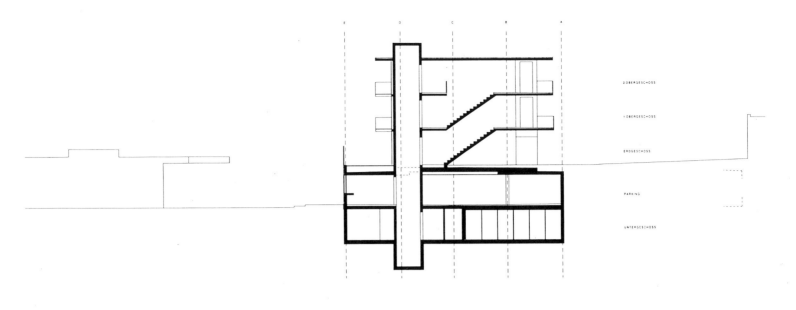

Section through communication core

A modular system was used for the construction of the apartment block. The structure is concrete and the walls are painted prefabricated fibreboard panels. The use of a varied range of colours shows the nature of the materials used.

The entrances to the dwellings stand out from the facade plane, and the adjacent voids give the dwellings privacy.
The garage is placed using the slope between the two facades.

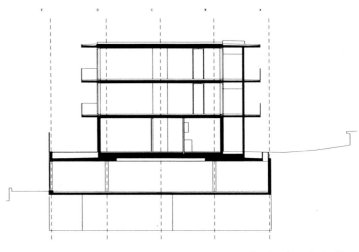

Section through dwellings

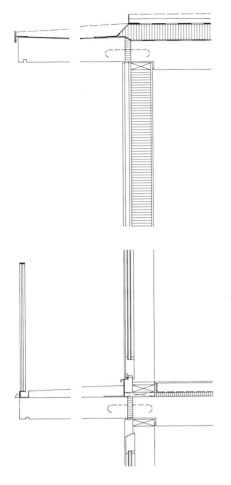

Construction detail of the facade

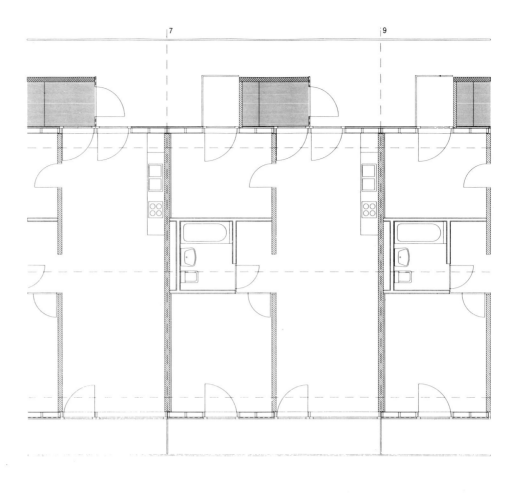

Plan of one of the dwellings

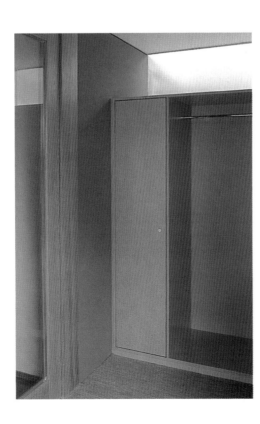

Splitterwerk
Complex Red Tree Frog
Bürmooss, Austria

These twelve housing units were set on the northern edge of the plot in the midst of a beech grove. Any sacrifices to the woodland had to be compensated by new planting. In creating access paths, terracing and parking lots, efforts were made to maintain the permeability of the soil. A further requirement was the application of an economical and ecological construction system.

Both the positioning of the building and the layout of the interiors seek to make the most of the natural sunlight and save energy. The generously glazed living areas and bedrooms are situated along the southern strip of the elongated volume. On the northern band are the foyers, kitchens and ancillary facilities, on the inner side of a long communal space which concentrates the circulation routes while serving as a thermal cushion for the apartments. The two-story building adapts to the slope of the site in such a way that the dwellings are terraced, although the continuous roof line restores the formal unity. Each unit is different and the typologies range from small apartments to duplexes. All are accessed from the communal space along the north facade. This three metre wide corridor is spacious enough to comfortably fit the steps that constitute the actual circulation route and a parallel strip of vegetation, besides the longitudinal footbridge that provides access to the second-floor homes and the perpendicular catwalks that lead to the lookouts projecting from the outer wall. These glazed openings and the longitudinal skylight turn the north corridor into a pleasant space to hang around. The strip of vegetation lining the inner facade adds to the environmental quality of the complex and helps to ensure the privacy of the rooms situated along this corridor. The south facade's cladding of red- and orange-painted timber strikes a contrast with the surrounding vegetation and with the concrete wall that closes the building to the north.

Photographs: Paul Ott

144

Oriented north-south, the long block follows the slope of the land, so the dwellings are stepped.
An economical and ecological construction system was used to minimise the impact on the beech grove.

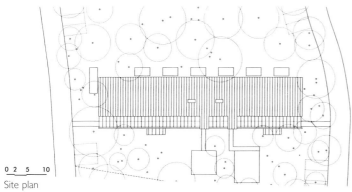

Site plan

Both the position of the building and the layout of the interiors seek to make the most of the natural sunlight, saving energy. The living areas and bedrooms receive sunlight from their situation along the southern strip of the elongated volume. On the northern side are the foyers, kitchens and ancillary facilities, on the inner side of a long communal space which serves as a thermal cushion for the apartments.

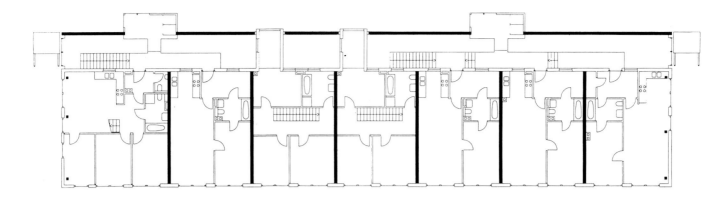

First floor plan

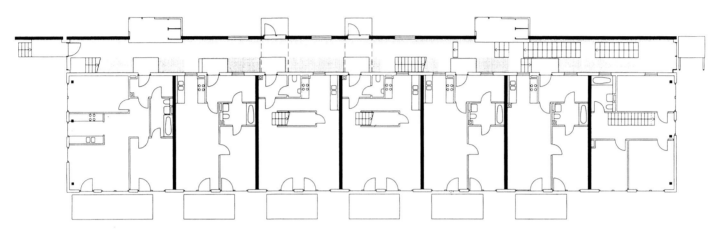

Access floor plan

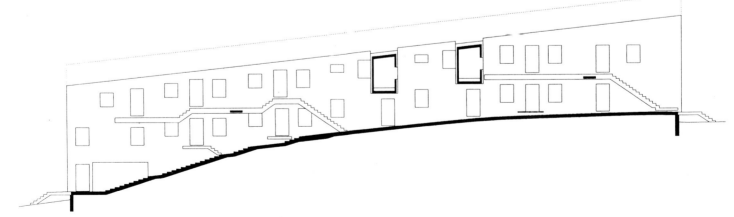

Basement plan   0 1 2   4

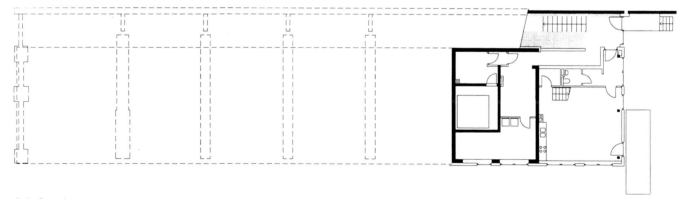

Longitudinal section

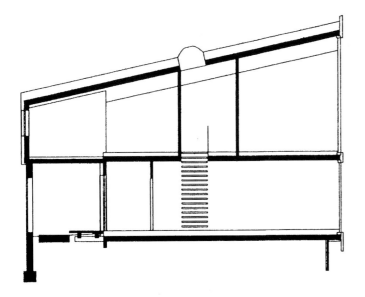

Cross-sections

The south facade, treated with red and orange coloured wood, marks a sharp contrast with the environment of the wood and the sober concrete wall that closes the opposite side.

147

A three-metre wide circulation gallery is placed along the north facade. A series of openings-viewpoints perforates the concrete wall that closes the gallery.

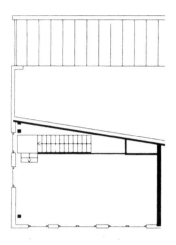

Upper level floor plan

Dietricht Fink & Thomas Jocher
Two multifamily dwellings
Regensburg, Germany

The two wooden structures were built within the inner courtyard of a landmarked housing estate dating back to 1925, at the southern border of the city of Regensburg. The main intention of the intervention was to add a contemporary construction to the existing estate while maintaining the identity of the place. The result is two structures that interfere minimally with the green courtyard. The ground floor is punctured and allows views through both buildings.

The structures are smooth and cubical, with repetitive openings. They relate to the surrounding houses along the streets. Their material language makes a connection to the garden sheds in the courtyard. The two buildings form a new yard into which the four public stairwells and the communal facilities are oriented. There are twelve one-bedroom apartments and four two-bedroom duplex apartments. Each apartment is organised across the building, providing contact to the front yard as well as the garden. The structures were built without basement —storage rooms · are located on the ground floor and on the landings of the stairs. The structures were designed on the principles of wood frame construction, and prefabrication of most parts helped to cut construction time to just four months.

Just a few materials dominate the appearance of the houses, each one used in its natural surface texture. In the intention to match the ratio of openings and walls of the landmarked old housing, an outer skin of narrow larch boards was designed to stretch across the open staircases, thus not articulating them on the outside. Filtered light passes through this skin into the staircases during the day, while at night the artificial lighting articulates the voids on the facade and illuminates the yard. Smooth plywood in large sheets was used only where the cubes are cut open, in the areas of direct contact between the building and its inhabitants.

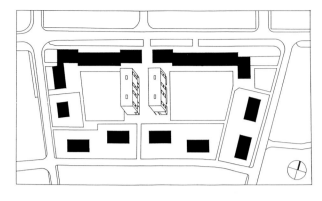

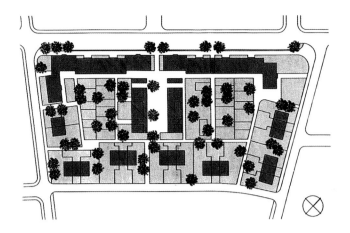

Site plan

The geometric purity of the two smooth, wholly wood-clad octagonal blocks with recurring openings contributes to their silent adaptation to the pre-existing natural environment.

0 0.5 1 2   North elevation

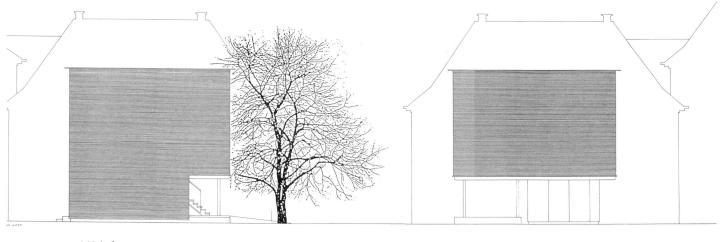

East elevation  0 0.5 1 2

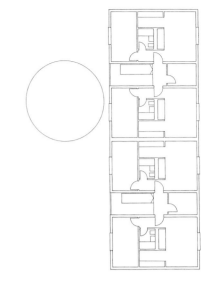

Second floor plan

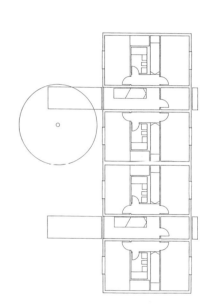

First floor plan

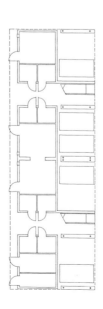

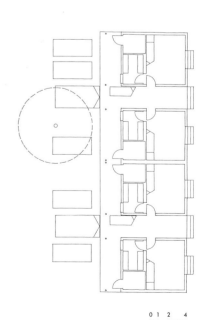

Ground floor plan

0 1 2 4

Cross-section   0 1 2   4

In order to conceal the articulation of the open stairways, their openings were covered with wooden slats. This allows light to filter into the interior.

Herrmann & Bosch

Collegienhaus

Marbach am Neckar, Germany

The Schiller-National museum, standing on the edge of the cliff of the Neckar valley, is a spiritual and structural focal point that dominates the landscape. Through its structural form the building of the German Literature Archive marks the boundaries of the site, maintaining the necessary distance from the neighbouring Museum.

The existing views over the valley from the front court of the museum are left unspoiled. A formal dependence of the layout of the new building on the existing museum building was not a feature of the design. Instead of a simple emulation in form and material, respect for this great historic building demands a contemporary interpretation and attitude in the task of designing the residential building.

Strengthened by the curved form of the ground plan, differentiated free zones emerge in combination with the interior spaces and, according to the situation of the observer, the form of the building becomes perceptible to different extents.

It was the wish of the German Schiller Society to build a house for individual accommodation and open encounters, for authors, guests and congress members who come to Marbach am Neckar from Germany and abroad to research and work on the literary sources in the German Literature Archive.

The architects found that the metaphors of the hotel, the guesthouse, the youth hostel and the monastery did not provide a suitable image for the desired atmosphere of the community residence in a Collegienhaus.

The buildings are set in a row on the undulating terrain. Stairs, landings and niches in the building permit unrestricted circulation and the chance meeting of the guests. The radial layout of all the apartments creates trapeziform interior spaces which provide freedom in the layout of the ground plans, sleeping area, dining area, work area, living space, and sanitary facilities.

Photographs: Christian Kandzia

The museum, situated on the edge of the cliff, marks the boundaries of the site and dominates the visual environments.

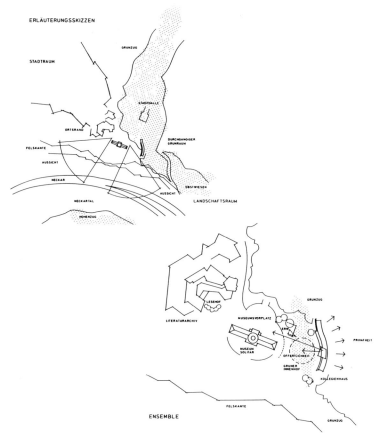

Site plan

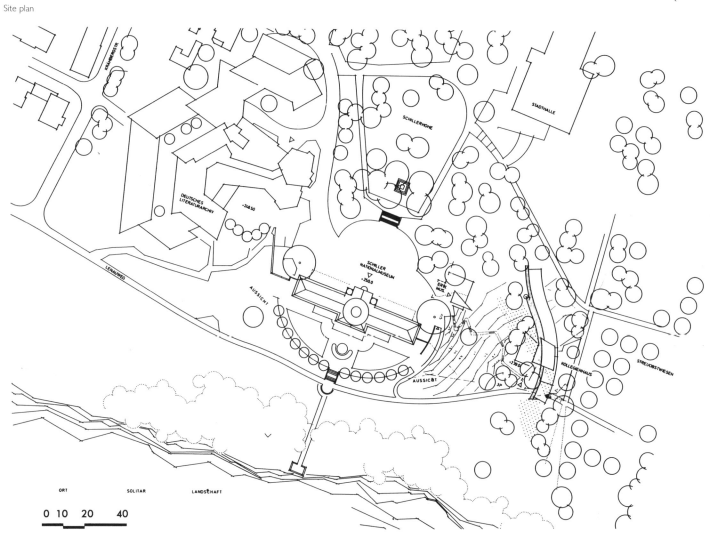

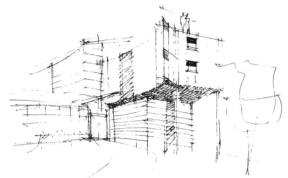

Due to the characteristic topography of the site, which is dominated by the presence of fruit trees, the design was strongly rooted in contemporary architecture with hardly any reference to the past.

West elevation

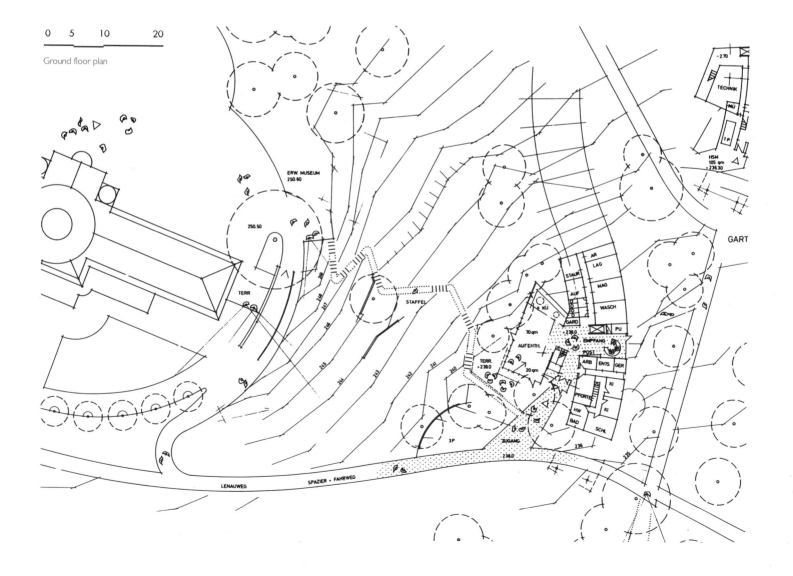

0 5 10 20

Ground floor plan

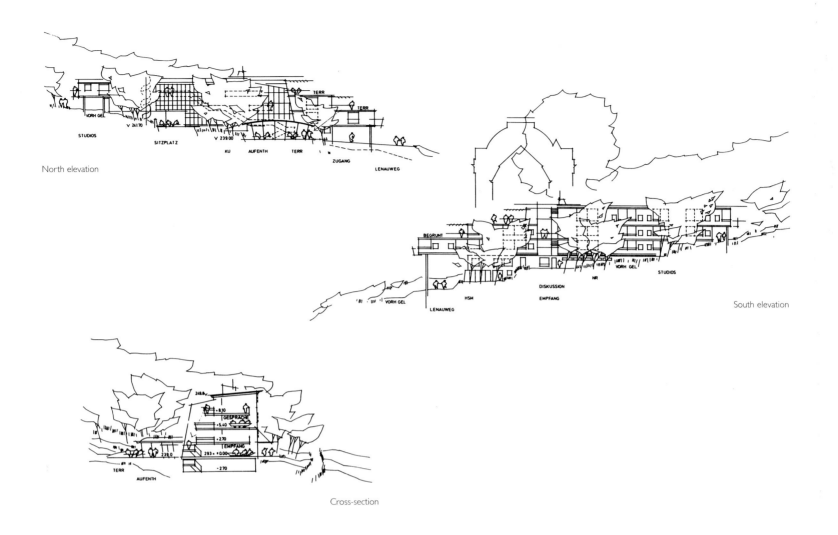

North elevation

South elevation

Cross-section

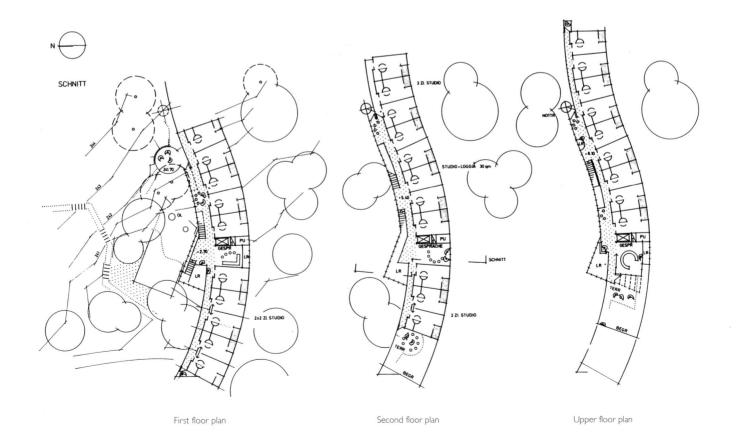

First floor plan

Second floor plan

Upper floor plan

In the interior of the four-storey building the staircases, landings and niches provide for very fluid circulation and the opportunity for encounter between guests and congress members from different countries.

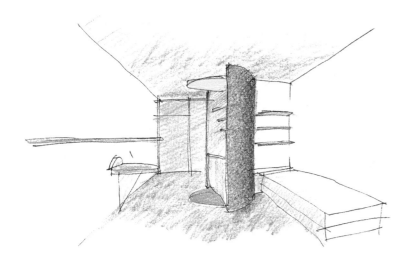

The radial layout of the apartments forms trapezoidal interior spaces that give full liberty in the arrangement of the different facilities.

In the interior of the apartments the spaces were distributed so as to create environments of study that are very compact and coherent.

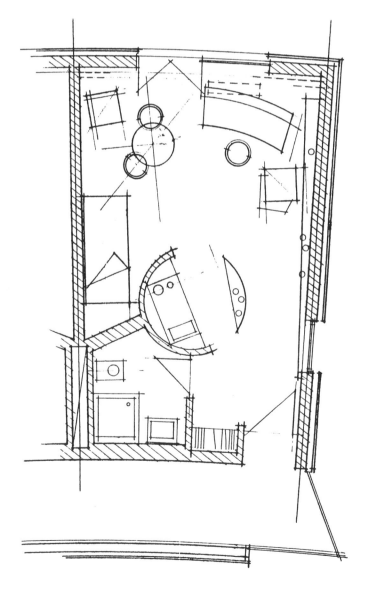

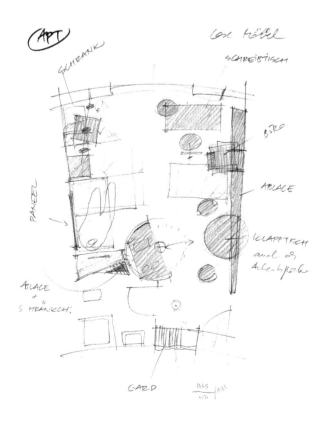

Type plan of the apartments

Carlo Baumschlager & Dietmar Eberle

Multi-storey housing in Nüzinders

Nüzinders, Austria

Fifteen apartments in Nüzinders are accommodated in two blocks which are placed on a tight site and share marvellous views. The area is dominated by an unstructured mix of single-family houses. The architects have made a clear statement which provides a strong contrast to the surroundings: a severe cubic architecture which elegantly balances the jump in scale by stepping the building elements and articulating them into two volumes.

The apartments have tenant's gardens, winter gardens, loggias and roof terraces and were individually adapted to the requirements of the residents.

The buildings themselves are simple, elegant and clear, and maintain a certain distance from their dubious surroundings. The flat roof, an unusual element of this region, emphasises the architecture's cubic character, especially on the street side. In the case of the larger, long, dramatically stepped block, the winter gardens at the rear emerge as sculptural ele-

ments; in the smaller building the inserted loggia is the element which provides a similar sculptural quality. Baumschlager and Eberle selected a façade solution that is highly unusual in terms of cubic architecture. They gave their buildings a cladding of larch shingles. In this region shingles are a traditional material which have proved their worth and their long-lasting quality in the difficult climatic conditions that prevail at this altitude. However, they have only rarely occurred in the vocabulary of contemporary architecture, one example being a very fine single-family house built in Bregenz by the same architects. In this project too they demonstrated that shingles do not inevitably lead to an earthy rusticality or to regional kitsch.

The decision to build multi-storey housing in this most unurban environment was a risky one, but the articulation into two elements turned out to be an important and correct decision, as is also, quite obviously, the facade solution.

Photographs: Christian Richters

0 1 2 4

South elevation

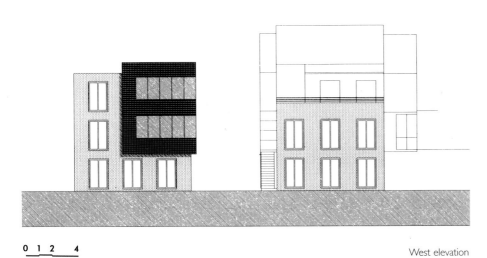

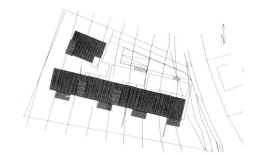

The project is divided into two blocks of staggered apartments that give the whole a sculptural aspect. These volumes are articulated by means of a small green area which serves as an access area to the dwellings.

0 1 2 4

West elevation

In accordance with the identity of this region, the facade was clad with small wooden panels. On the south side, the staircases and balconies are closed with panels of translucent glass so that the entrance to each apartment is visible from the exterior.

0 1 2 4

Second floor plan

Shigeru Ban

Hanegi Forest in Tokyo

Tokyo, Japan

A random group of twenty-seven large trees remained on this land in a quiet residential district in Tokyo. What was required in the programme was to build an apartment house cutting down none of the existing trees, while at the same time staying within a restricted budget. Steel-frame construction was adopted to avoid damaging the trees. It was understood that if the column arrangement were to follow the random positions of the trees, the column and beam sizes as well as the joints would have to be diversified and the construction costs would become much higher; for this reason a geometrical grid system which would not interfere with the trees was sought.

Consequently, a grid of regular triangles (4 metres to a side) was found as a system which can ensure structural stability while providing suitably-sized living areas even with the arbitrary cut-offs of columns, beams and girders. This system also provides horizontal rigidity and a struc-ture which allows free spatial composition with proper cantilevering of the floor slabs, even when the spaces around the trees are hollowed out in circular or oval shapes. Each of the eleven apartment units is built in a terrace-house style which occupies the floors from the first to the third. This style makes fireproof construction unnecessary between floors and makes it possible to expose the real structural system. In addition, it provides the inhabitants with views of the natural setting on several levels. Full-height furniture units sandwiched between the floor slabs help subdivide the apartment units with compositional clarity and high sound-insulating efficiency. In order to enhance the image of the forest, the first-floor pilotis area is made transparent with only the entrance doors remaining at that level. Mirrored glazing in the private rooms reflects and amplifies the images of the trees.

Photographs: Hiroyuki Hirai

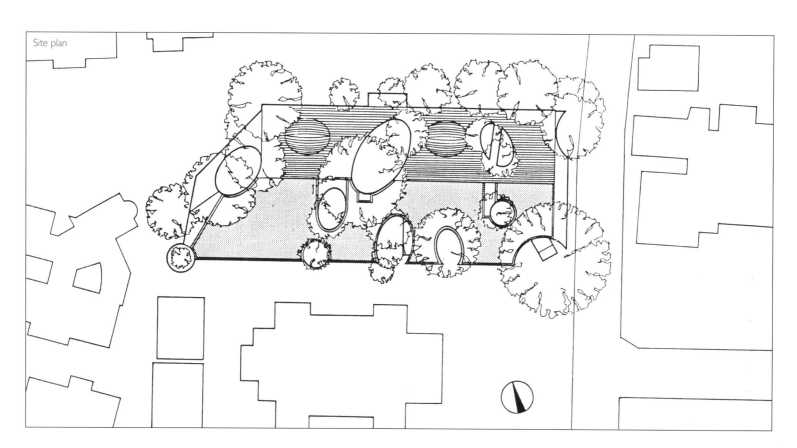

Site plan

Located in a quiet residential district of Tokyo, the building designed by Shige-ru Ban houses eleven apartments distributed on three levels within a volume of unusual geometry. Some of the trees belonging to the wood in which the building is inserted have been left in the oval inner courtyards.

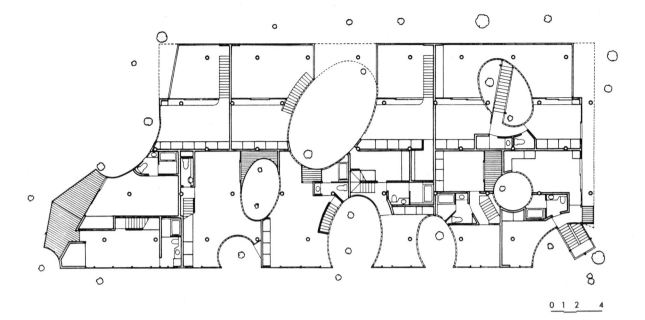

Third floor plan

0 1 2 4

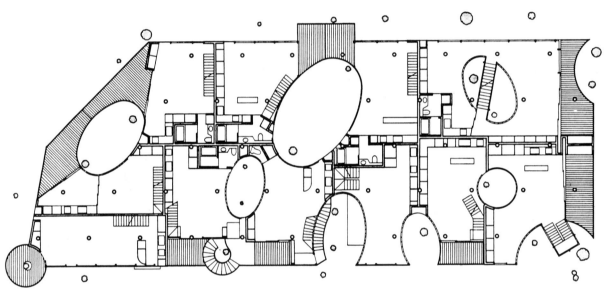

Second floor plan

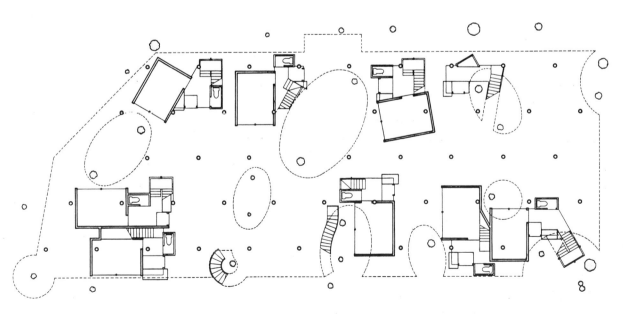

First floor plan

In the interior, the apartments are warm, minimal spaces bathed in the elegance that characterises the work of this Japanese architect, In the large photograph, a view of the living room of one of the dwellings. On the left, a detail of a skylight of a type B apartment.

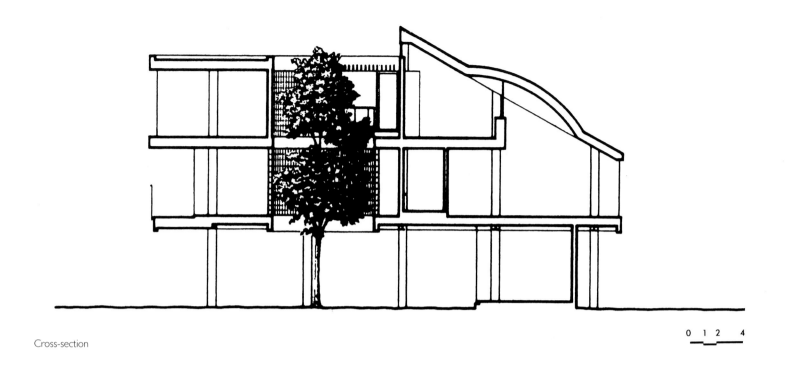

Cross-section

0 1 2 4

In the interior of the apartments, the large windows combine the transparent glass panels of the facades facing the exterior with the curved glass brick walls that hide the staircases and access walkways to the exterior terraces and that face the inner courtyard.

179

Theresienstieg Herbert-Weichmann-Strasse

Hamburg, Germany

The property is designed as part of an old parkland. A 200 year old beech tree with a wide crown stands in the centre of the property. Around this tree, cubic volumes form two buildings. A gap at the narrowest part conserves the microclimate.

The building volumes have a different materiality and a varied relationship of apertures and solid surfaces. The glass volume on the ground floor is for office use. The large volumes of wood and render seem to hover over it. They contain five apartments. Render and copper mark the penthouse areas on the roof. The large-size laminated wood panels of the facade were impregnated for fire protection and then stained red-orange. Together with the green of the copper, this colourfulness marks the change of the building structures along Herbert-Weichmann-Strasse.

The homogeneity of the single cubic volumes is reinforced by the facades: the windows are placed flush in the wood and render facade, so the outer skin remains flat and unplastic. At the rear of the building, an apartment stretches over three levels with a total of 260 sqm. At the front there are four apartments with 100 to 150 sqm.

In the ground plan of the apartments, the communal area (hall, dining room, kitchen, living room) is sharply separated from the individual rooms (bedrooms, bathrooms). The offices have an open plan with structural elements in the centre. Parking space for 12 cars is provided in the basement.

The existing vegetation dictated the landscaping. New trees were added in parts, and light wooden bridges mark the accesses to the dwellings.

Photographs: Oliver Heissner/ Contur

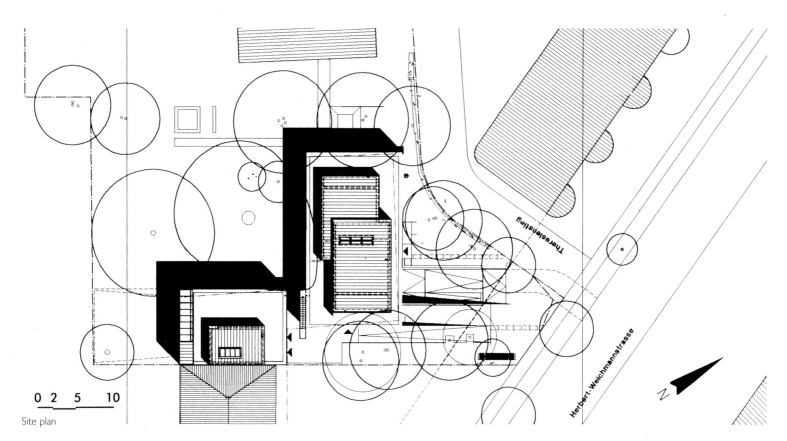

0 2 5 10

Site plan

The front volume, with its completely glazed ground floor, was clad with red spruce boards in vertical strips. The absence of horizontal joints avoids deterioration due to damp.

South-west elevation

South-east elevation

North-west elevation

North-east elevation

Cross-section

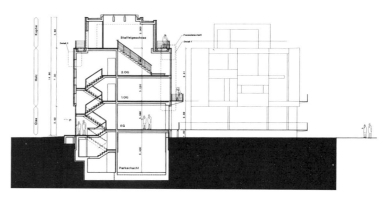

The two blocks have different relations between voids and solids. The rear volume is white-rendered at the top and grey on the opaque panels of the ground floor. The wooden platform that joins the lower level is the only common element to the two parts.

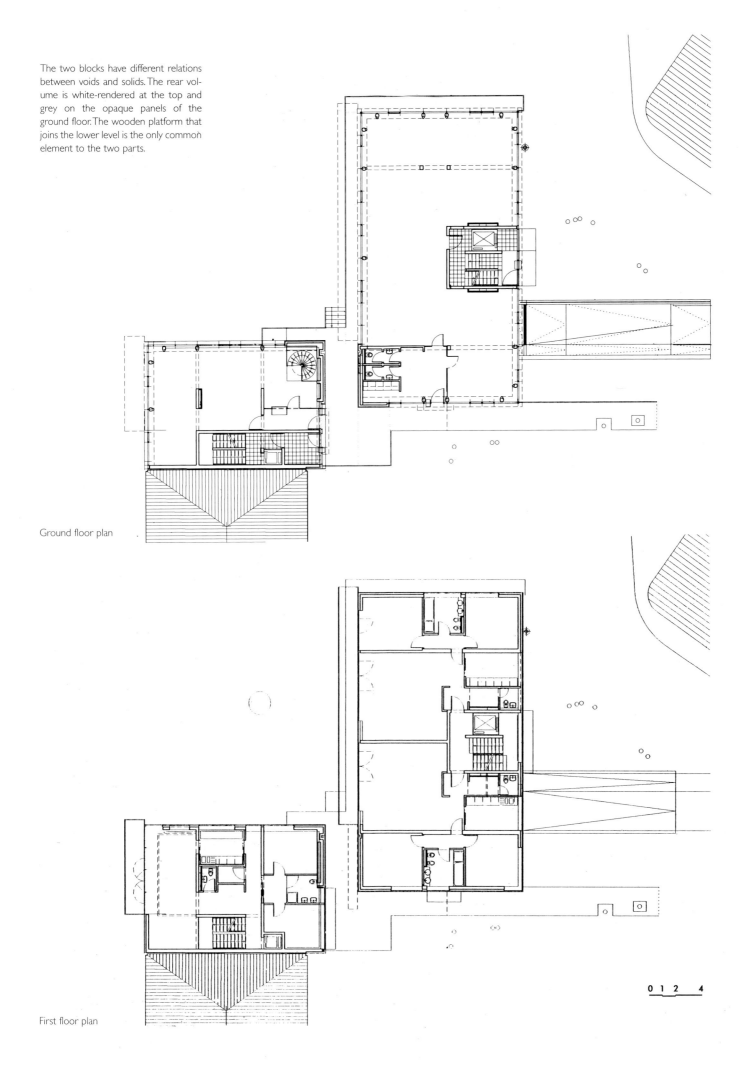

Ground floor plan

First floor plan

0 1 2 4

184

Second floor plan

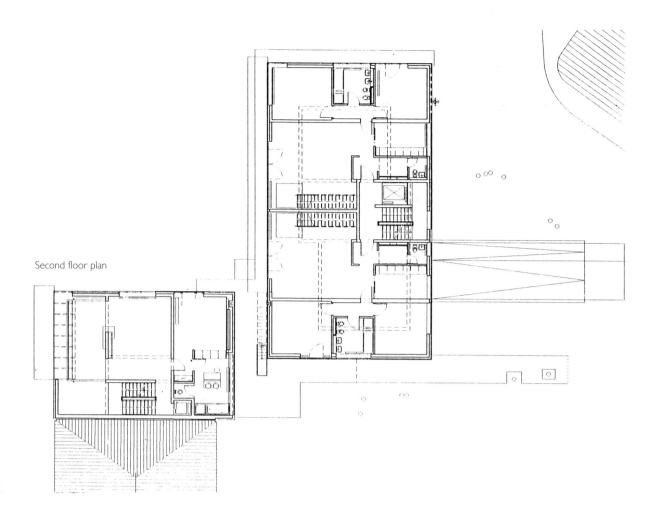

The plot is dominated by an impressive copper beech that stands in the centre and made it necessary to divide the programme into two parts, leaving between them a crack for the ventilation of the tree.

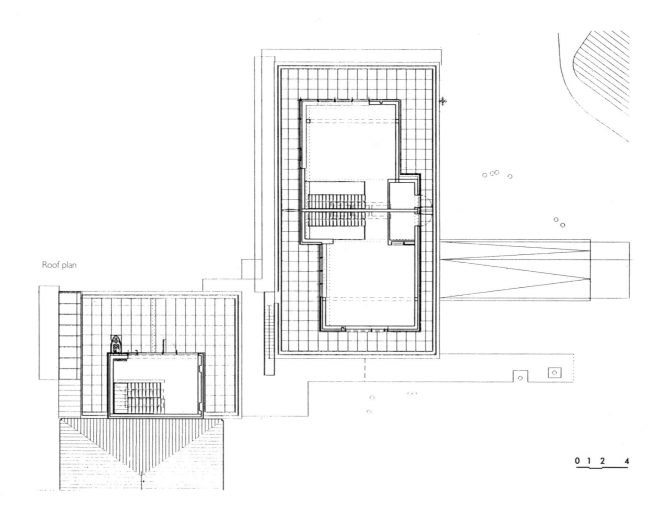

Roof plan

0 1 2 4

Jean Nouvel

Apartements in Tours-Ilot

Tours, France

This city building incorporates some novelties. First, being privately promoted, certain approaches cease to be experimental and come to form part of market demands of housing. Second, the building's mixture of commercial and residential uses, which is the attention paid to its urban implantation.

Unlike the previous projects, in each of which the programme is distributed in two longitudinal volumes, this is a single tablet placed parallel to the street. Yet the scheme is essentially the same. Circulation is through an exterior system of metal stairs and ramps attached to the rear facade of the building, and both the dwellings of the top floors and the offices below are arranged transversally in relation to the narrow bay, an optimal position in terms of ventilation and natural lighting. The double-height ground floor is occupied by the city's Tourist Office as well as by technical premises serving the Convention Centre. With one of its walls painted entirely in Yves Klein's famous blue, the foyer crosses through the building, allowing access to the rear circulation system. The articulations in the floor plan and the section give rise to a wide variety of apartment types within the building but all have a space between the living room and the street facade, separated by a foldable element. On the top floor, this space becomes a continuous balcony.

The only differentiation made patent on the street-side facade is that between the upper residential body, expressed through a rigorous modular system dominated by the horizontal line, and the commercial-use plinth, formed by vertical glass panels without joinery. Shades that can be rolled up and down at will give a sense of movement to this facade.

This double page gives a clear indication of the singular features of the facade. This foreshortened view of the street, with the Conference Centre in the background, shows the strict modulation of the facade.

On the left: The frameless windows on the ground floor break the horizontality of the facade. The roller blinds provide the exterior of the building with rhythm.

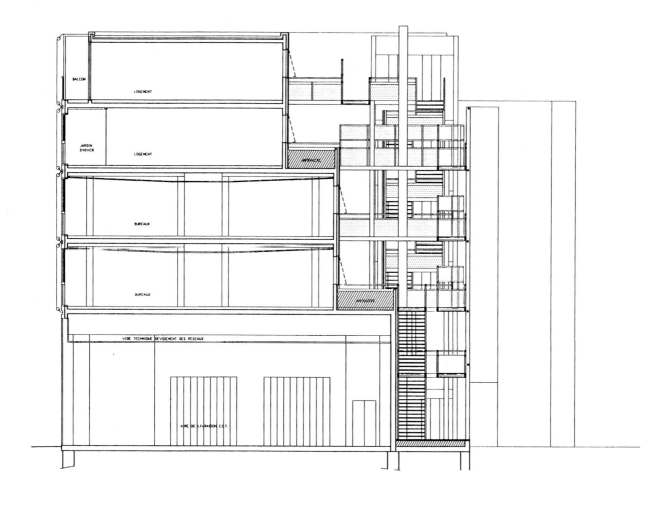

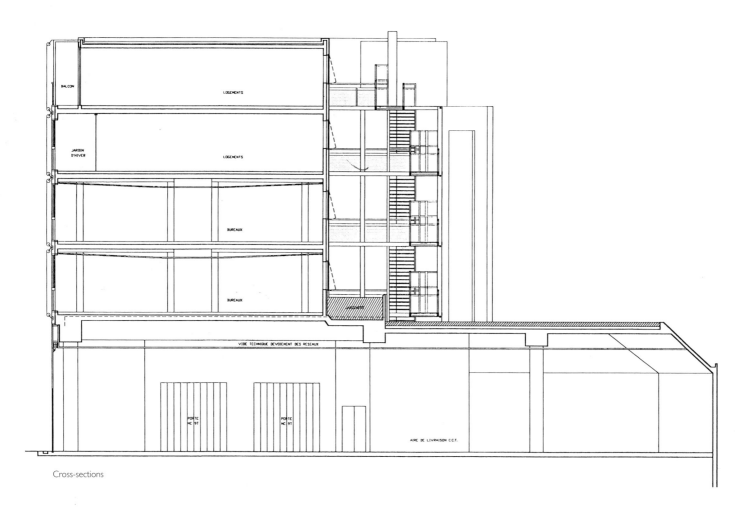

Cross-sections

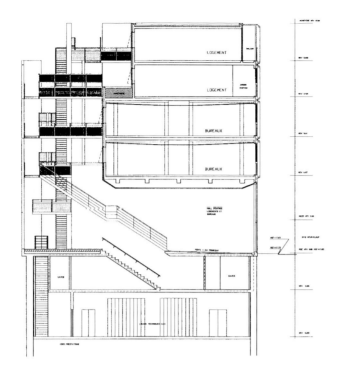
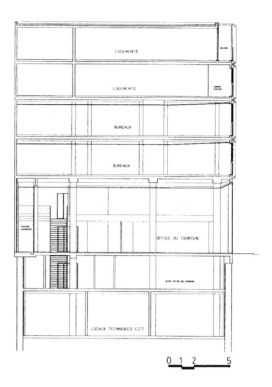

View of the entrance hall, with one of the
walls painted entirely in Yves Klein blue.

Ground floor

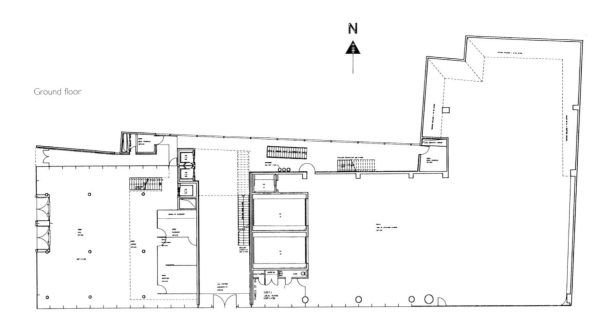

Floor model

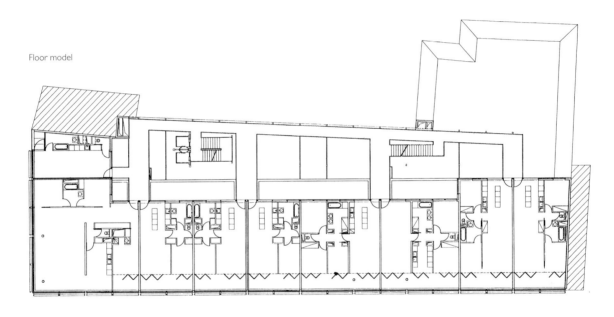

Upper level

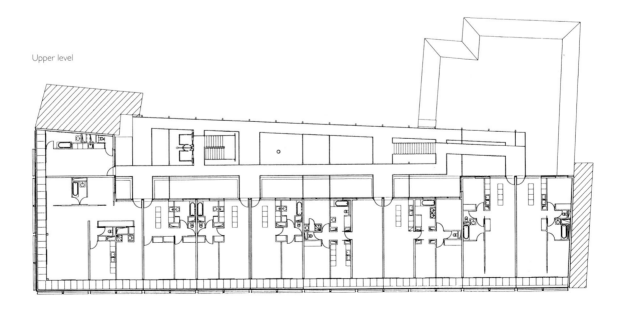

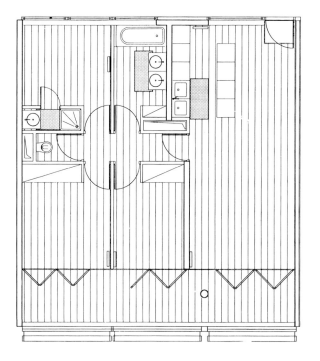

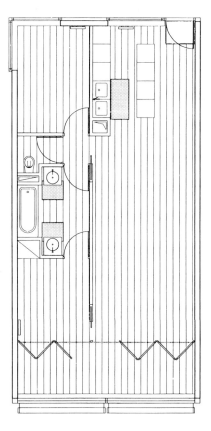

Model of floors of accommodation

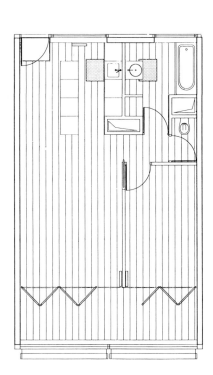

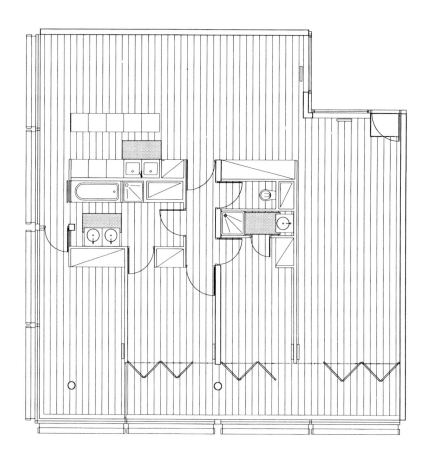

Phillippe Gazeau
Postmen's flats
Paris, France

"La Poste" commissioned the organisation in charge of building welfare homes for its employees PLA (prêt locatif aidé) flats for young postmen arriving to work in Paris. The Post Office wanted to give them the chance to live in flats in the city centre, their place of work, so they would not have to make long journeys on the underground.

Although most of the dwellers were single, special "studios" and two-room flats had to be built for the married couples. An additional area for temporarily accommodating children was provided for young couples.

The land allocated to Phillippe Gazeau was on rue de l'Ourcq in the 19th arrondissement, a working class district whose population density increased dramatically in the sixties and seventies. The district had no stylistic identity: It was almost entirely constructed this century.

Gazeau skillfully cut the building in two. This gave him two separate blocks to work with: one was 3.50 metres wide and 15 metres long, and was used for accommodating a "studio", the other was 7.50 metres wide. The building was therefore constructed around an empty space, a fault, defined by a large staircase, which does not overhang on the roadside but juts out at the back of the building.

The same attention to detail has been paid to both the interiors and exteriors, although more "precious" materials have been used for the exteriors to give the building the kind of dignity that is usually lacking in welfare buildings. Considerable attention has also been paid to the choice of materials: black brick, glass, aluminium and wood are skillfully combined. The facade overlooking the road is a composition of large glazed surfaces fitted with sliding aluminium panels to conceal the interior.

Photographs: Jean-Marie Monthiers

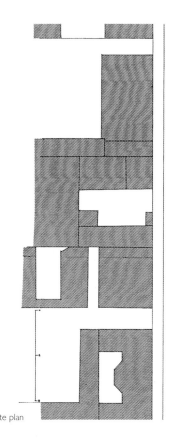

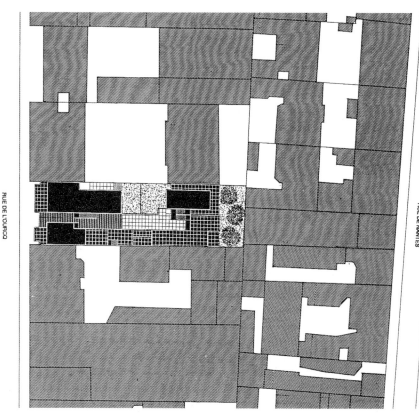

Site plan

196

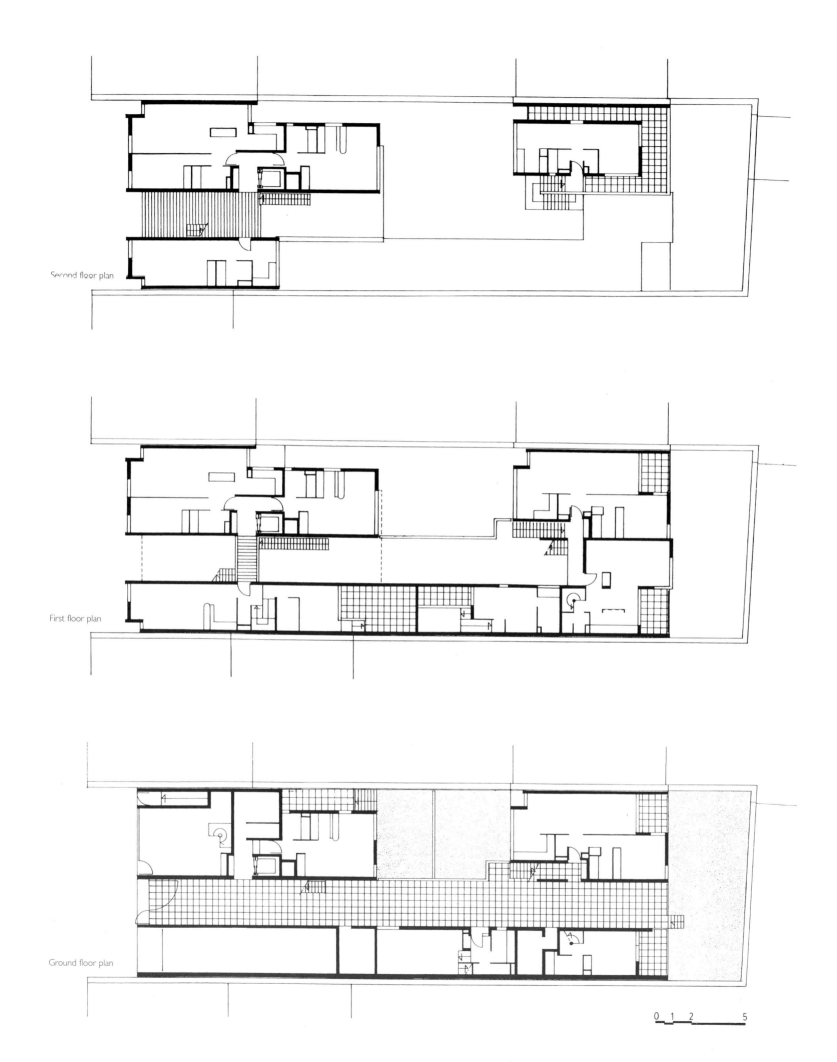

Second floor plan

First floor plan

Ground floor plan

0 1 2 5

This staircase leads into the buildings and constructs a shared space where people can congregate, exchange a few words or just stop and watch what is going on below.
The same attention to deal has been paid to both the interiors and exteriors.

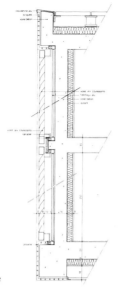

Constructive detail of the facade

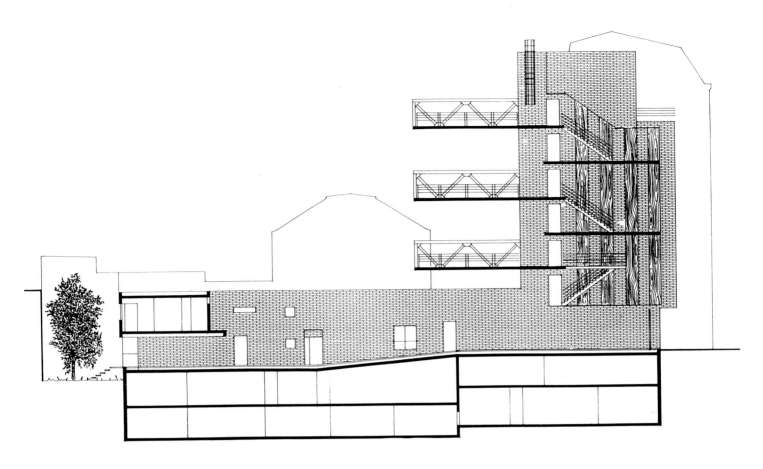

Philippe Madec
Logements à Paris 20
Paris, France

This district of Paris contains low buildings housing workshops and warehouses and studios, small suburban houses, and above all blocks of flats from the sixties. With this reconstruction Philippe Madec has chosen a new interpretation of the typical Parisian residence with its rows of windows, shutters, balconies and zinc roofs.

In the result, quite another architecture presents itself to the observer. The homogeneous facades are characterised by the wooden louvers, the concrete bands of the floor slabs and the full-height windows that provide maximum lighting in the interiors. 21 residential units of different sizes were created, some are organised as maisonettes, with 25 parking places in the basement. Due to the sloping terrain of Rue Pixerecourt the cars have ground level access to the garage, which is partially open to the garden. The apartments are housed in two independent buildings on the site, which is divided into two parts. The larger

and higher building with 17 apartments is to the south-west, on Rue de la Duée, whereas the smaller one with four apartments was inserted on Rue Pixerecourt. This smaller building is in turn subdivided into a grey rendered block giving onto the street, and a two-storey building giving onto the yard. With his decision to construct two buildings on the extremely narrow plot, Madec wanted to give the apartments the best possible orientation and to create an interior garden. Moreover, he wished to respect the scale of the neighbouring buildings to the north and west.

Especially the hall areas that surround the round stairway and the elevator of the main building, but also the ground plans of some apartments, are full of corners and extremely narrow. It was quite obviously a priority here to make full use of a minimum area, so the quality of the apartments is unfortunately reduced to the generous windows and the excellent finish.

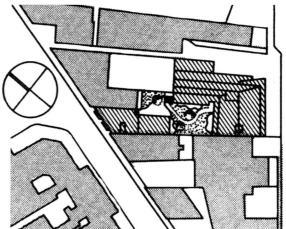

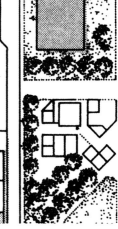

The project is organised around a small interior garden that occupies the centre of the plot. An underground car park is situated beneath it.

The apartments are divided into two differentiated volumes, one of five floors in the side facing the street and one of two floors on the side facing the garden.

Ground floor plan

Typical floor plan

The dwellings receive a great deal of natural light through generous openings in the facade. A system of sliding wooden blinds of red cedar filters the incoming light. The wooden blinds and the horizontal strips of prefabricated concrete help to compose the facade formally.

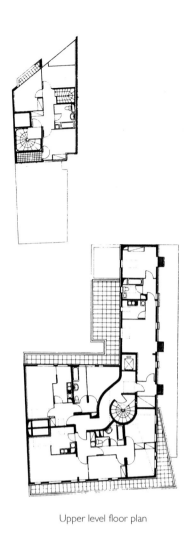

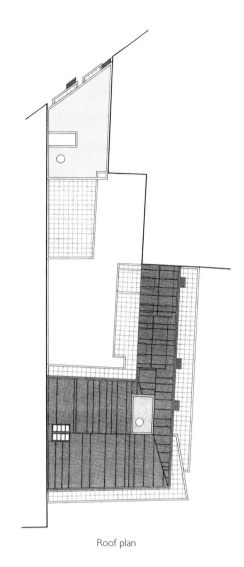

Upper level floor plan

Roof plan

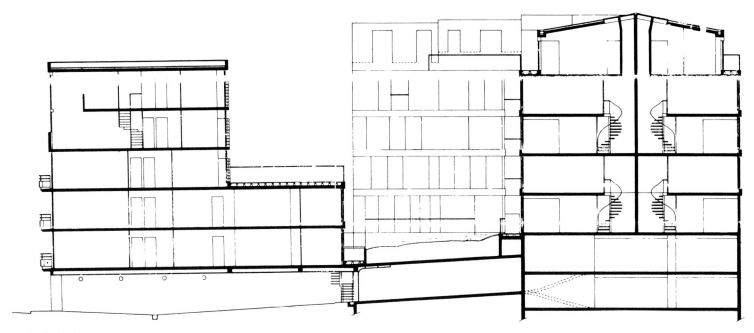

Longitudinal section

Eduard Broto

Edificio Plurifamiliar

Terrassa (Barcelona), Spain

Located in Terrassa, near Barcelona, the building occupies a square site, with 10 dwellings distributed on three floors and three small studios housed in an independent volume. The building shows a striking front facade on inverted tapered pillars lined with polished stainless steel, a material that is repeated in the frames of the entrance and the visors of the overhangs that stand out from the facade. From this side, the project is broken down into several elements.

A green marble open podium with columns sustains the building and raises it toward the west side to avoid the slope of the street. The slightly recessed entrance area is set behind a row of pillars; here all the glass was installed with concealed structural silicone, leaving it totally flush with the marble plane. Finally, the main volume of brickwork is modulated by means of a zig-zag play of openings. A sequence of twelve small quadrangular windows perforates and opens up this facade,

which protects the terrace of the apartments housed on the roof.

The side facades show a more introverted and hermetic version of the building, with forms of flush marble and brickwork with few openings, in which the frames of dark grey aluminium with horizontal slats stand out against the brickwork and ventilate the laundry areas of the three main floors. The composition of both facades includes at the sides the balconies of the rear facade and the extension of the marble podium, which houses the car park for residents.

The south-facing rear facade is of brickwork and white render, and is traversed in its whole length by three balcony levels with a structure of stainless steel and limited glass with dark coloured butyl.

Finally, a free-standing volume on the roof houses a suite and a multi-function space with an open ground plan and a glazed front, communicating with the apartments on the third level.

Photographs: Eugeni Pons

Main elevation

The lower part of the building functions as a plinth clad in green marble. As can be seen on this double page, the project also redesigned the street that flanks the building on the east side. Following the regulations on architectural barriers for the handicapped, the existing staircases were replaced with a flowing double ramp featuring a zig-zag pattern of perforated concrete elements that recalls the formal discourse of the main facade.

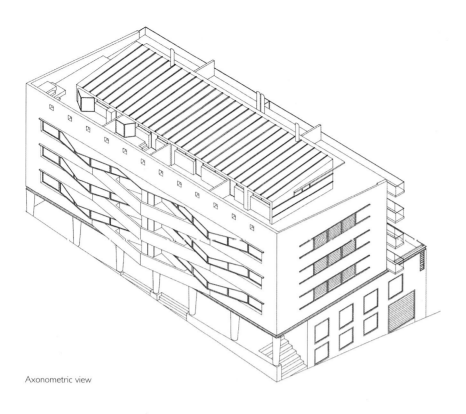

Axonometric view

The combination of brick and marble has a powerful presence in the project, as an expressive resource that marks a strong chromatic and formal contrast between the pedestal of the building and its main volume.

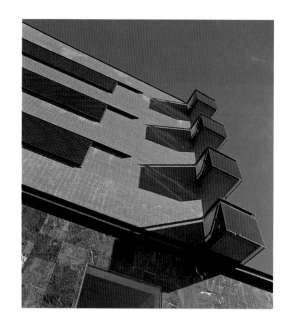

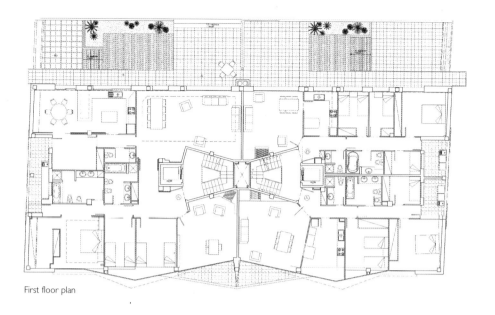

First floor plan

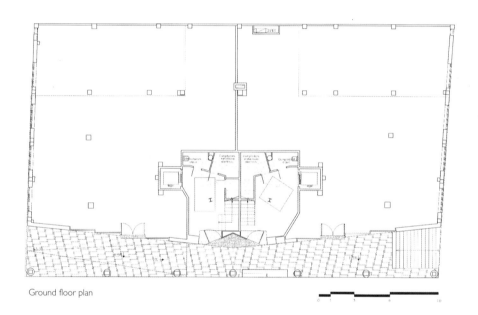

Ground floor plan

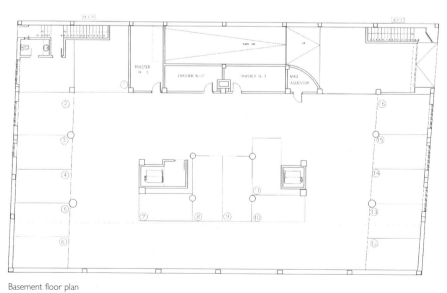

Basement floor plan

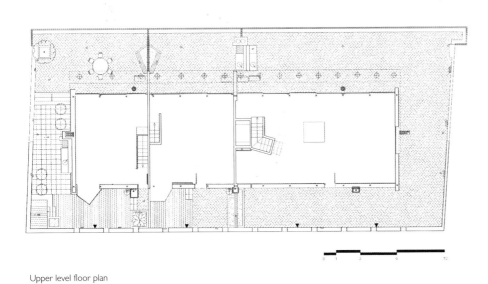

Upper level floor plan

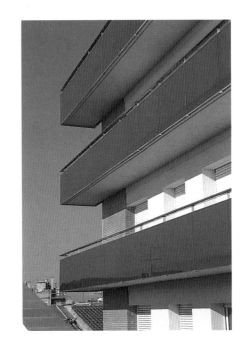

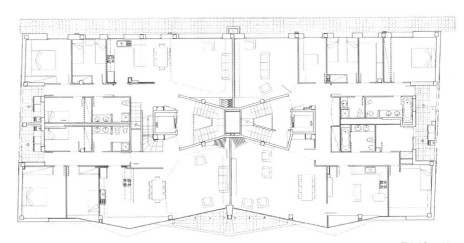

Third floor plan

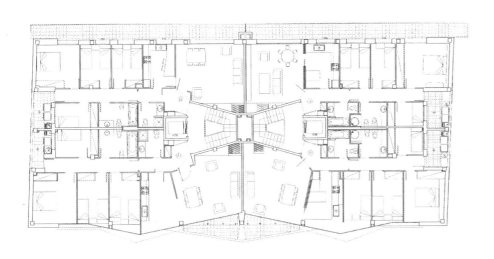

Second floor plan

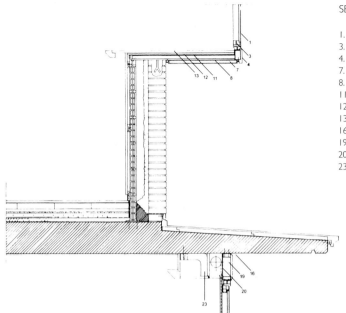

SECTION OF CALLE VALLHONRAT FACADE

1.   Safety glass
3.   Aluminium profiles with thermal insulation
4.   Painted aluminium sheet lining
7.   Extruded thermal insulation
8.   Steel plate
11. Waterproof butyl sheet
12. Damp-proof MDF
13. Wooden board with varnished cherry veneer
16. Smooth painted concrete
19. Polyurethane foam
20. Painted steel plate
23. Mineral wool insulation

The building is divided vertically into two clearly differentiated areas. This separation disappears in the car park, whose two floors are structured horizontally. The glass volumes of the three small apartments located in the roof are projected outward toward the terrace.

At the top, the roof of the three small apartments slopes in the opposite direction to that of the terrace wall. The wood of the flooring sharply contrasts with the white cladding of the terrace wall. The latter acts as a canvas for the daily changes of light.

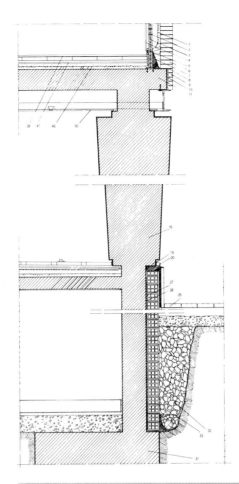

SECTION OF MAIN FACADE AND FIRST UNDERGROUND LEVEL

1. Thermal insulation applied in situ
2. Hollow brick wall
3. Solid metal profile
4. Cladding of wooden board with varnished cherry veneer
5. Flanders pine fillet treated in autoclave
6. Perforated brickwork
7. Impermeable sheet
8. Stainless mechanical anchor
9. Sheet T profile
10. Extruded thermal insulation
11. Grid slab
16. Reinforced concrete landing
19. Polyurethane seal
20. Spanish concrete
27. Delta drain sheet
28. Waterproof wall paint
29. Pavement tiles
32. Drainage gravel
33. Geo-textile filter
37. Reinforced concrete foundation
38. Glued parquet panels
41. Levelling sand
46. Krafft paper separator
50. False ceiling of ekume board

215

Christian Hauvette

166 Logements en ascenssion privée

Rennes, France

This project is located in an area very close to the town centre of Rennes. The planning regulations and the landscaping plan of the area were drawn up by the French architect Alexandre Chemetoff.

Christian Hauvette's intervention is based on the construction of a residential complex concentrated in three elevations on a large quadrangular site that is interrupted on its short side, facing the river Vilaine, in order to conserve a small red-stone dwelling that had been on the site for some time. According to Hauvette, this old building was a decisive element in the configuration of the crown of the new building: "The Brigitte house served as an argument for the crowning of the project. It was multiplied on the roofs in the form of armoured volumes of reddish copper, surrounded by large terraces". These house twelve maisonettes, with single-floor dwellings on the six lower levels.

The complex has two faces: it is more hermetic towards the exterior of the site, and more transparent and open toward the interior. On the street side, the building is protected from traffic noise by a metal structure that forms the support for the glass panels of the balconies and large awnings that provide protection from rain and sunlight.

The part facing the interior is configured by a mesh of polished concrete that forms wide balconies designed as boxes for plants and flowers. These form a vertical extension of the garden designed by Chemetoff, which occupies the centre of the plot above the underground car park.

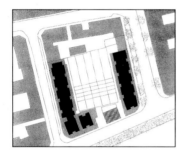

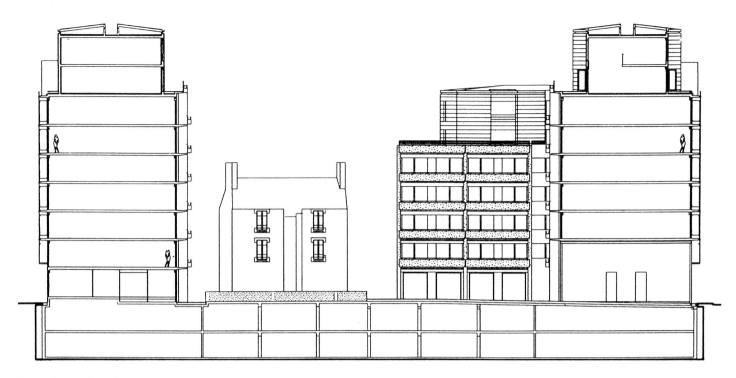

Cross-section from the garden

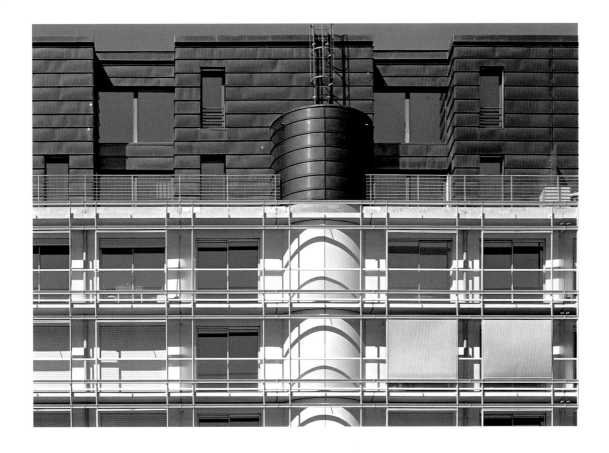

The facing page shows a front view of the facade of the complex facing the River Vilaine, with the small existing building between the two new volumes. The new volumes have six levels of single-floor dwellings and a double height area at the top housing twelve small duplex apartments that are expressed on the exterior in geometric elements clad with copper plate surrounded by balconies.

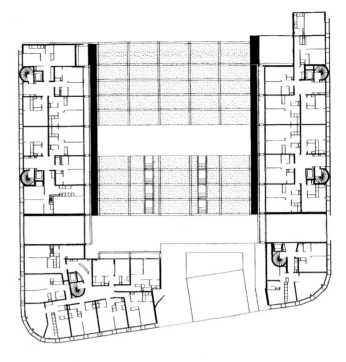

The project uses two types of facade. Towards the exterior, the building is protected against the noise of the street behind a metal structure that forms the support for the glass panels of the balconies and large awnings that provide protection from rain and sunlight.

The part facing the interior is configures by a mesh of polished concrete that forms wide balconies designed as flower boxes, which in the future could dress the facade with plants and flowers as a vertical extension of the garden.

The residential complex located in central Rennes embraces a quadrangular site whose interior is occupied by a raised garden

The U-shaped ground plan of the complex is interrupted at the shortest side in order to conserve a small red stone building that was already on the site.

Typical floor plan

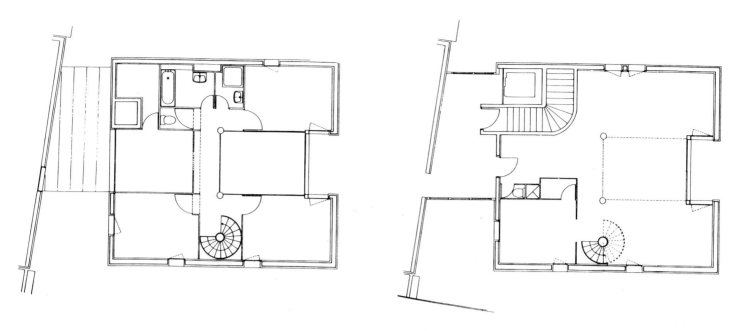

Ground floor and upper floor plans of the small duplex apartments located at the top of the complex.

Herzog & De Meuron

Apartments on a long and narrow lot

Basel, Switzerland

This commercial and apartment building was built on a parcel located within the city's medieval perimeters. Thus the long narrow measurements (23 by 6.3 metres) typical of medieval parcelling had to be accommodated. The architecture was strongly influenced by this parcel, which was utilised right to the back of the lot and exhibits a highly specific floor plan and section for life in a densely-built city. The apartments are grouped around a central courtyard aperture that opens on one side to the neighbouring parcel to the south. This side opening was not only intended to let light and sun reach the apartments but also to allow for the enjoyment of the branches of a large tree in the neighbour's yard. Like a periscope, the courtyard is recessed floor-by-floor to clearly separate the individual apartments.

The stairway has been separated from the elevator shaft to gain area for the central living space. The apartments are entered directly from the elevator. The stairs at the end of the parcel are an open construction, thus fulfilling the additional function of a small loggia.

On the ground floor, a two-story hallway leads from the street along the old parcel wall and allows access to the Swiss Fire Fighting Museum located in the back courtyard. The street facade is made completely of glass and is protected by a cast-iron curtain construction that can be folded back piece-by-piece at will. Wavy light slits lend the curtain construction a flowing textile-like feeling. While the construction hides the living space behind it, its heavy cast-iron material serves as a counter-weight protecting against the noisy street side. In form and material, the facade components are related to sewer grates and to the protective grills placed around the trees.

Photographs: Margherita Spiluttini

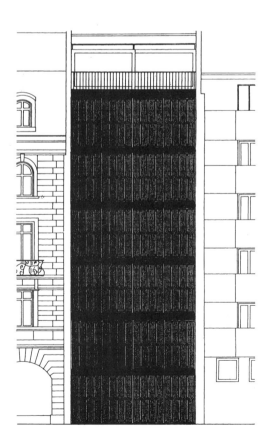

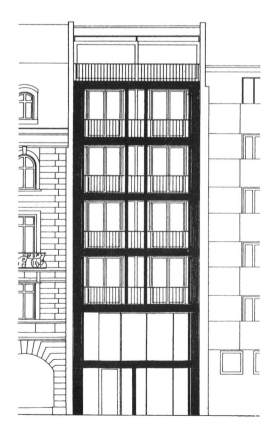

Front view of the main facade, characterised by the unusual cast iron curtain, which as it sways endows the whole scene with fluidity and dynamism. The detail below shows how the individual links of the curtain are joined together.
Left: Two elevations of the main facade, the first with the curtain totally shut and the second with it open. The photograph shows the total independence of the structure, as a result of which the residents can adapt it to their specific needs.

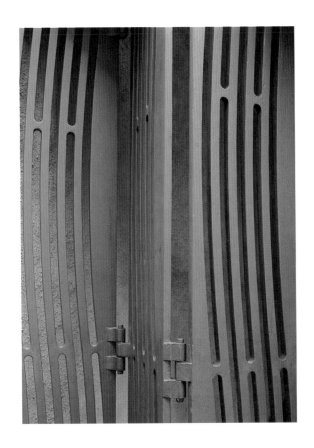

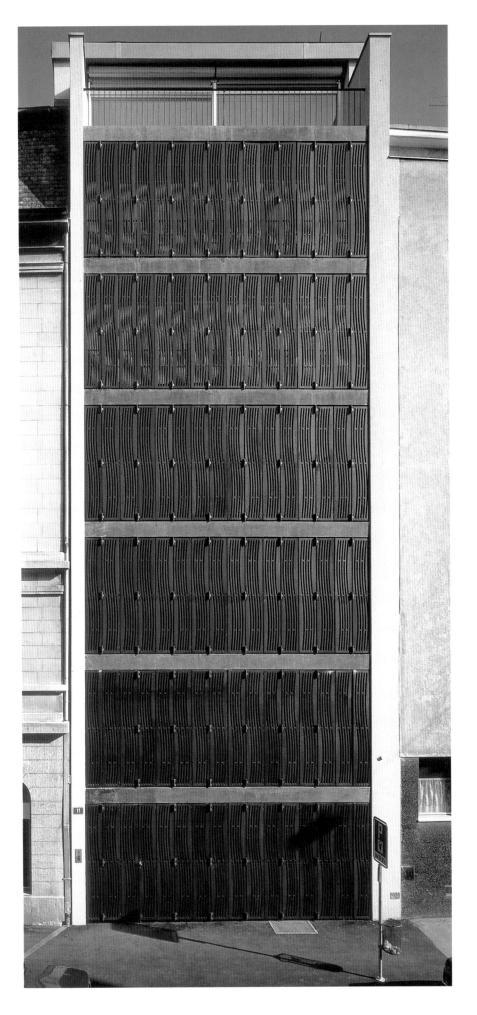

223

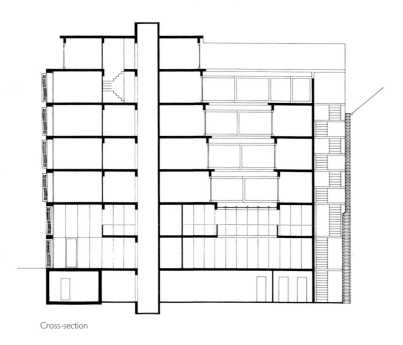

Cross-section

The apartments are grouped around a central courtyard, which is open to the south to take full advantage of natural light and the existence of a large tree standing nearby.

The apartments seen from the central courtyard. The outside walls are almost totally glazed, although here they are shown protected by wooden blinds.

224

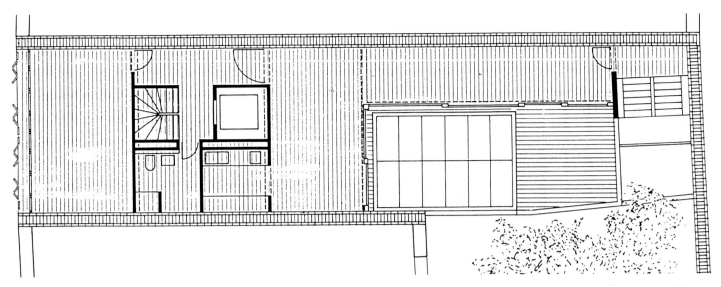

Fourth floor plan

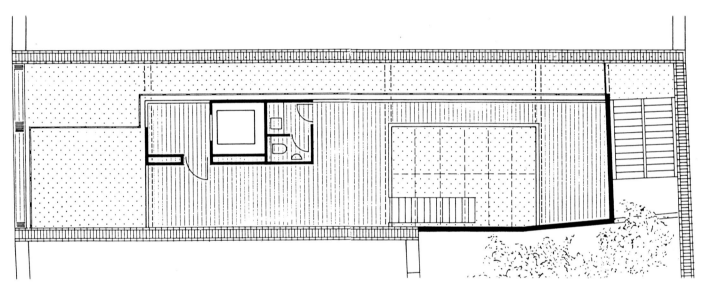

First floor plan

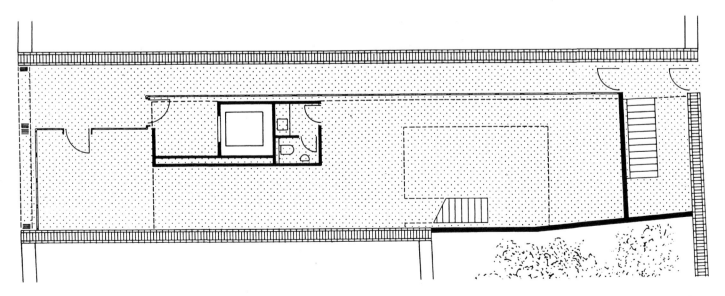

Ground floor plan

Two pictures showing the close relationship the interiors have with the exteriors: With the central courtyard (top) and with the street (bottom).
Next page: View of the entrance into one of the apartments

Josep Lluís Mateo

Viviendas en Torelló

Torelló, España

In the old part of the village, the building develops an active and generous relationship with the narrow and undulating street on which it is located. The functional mixture (dwellings on the upper floors; public services on the ground floor) makes it necessary to juxtapose technologies; to use structures consisting of brick walls for the dwellings and structures consisting of concrete pillars on the ground floor. Manipulating this fact, the solid upper part of the building seems to float over the street, where it extends the public space. The facade of the block displays all the contextualist stereotypes (long windows, balconies, etc.), trying to distort them without fully destroying the familiar images, which make communication possible.

Particularly surprising is the treatment of balconies and windows. The windows emerge from the facade plane and have a system of sliding panels on exposed rails.

Indeed, the intervention of Josep Lluís Mateo is an exploration of the traditional typological concepts and of contextualism, with the addition of new elements that without destroying the architectural essence of the surroundings give the building a clear and perfectly distinguishable identity.

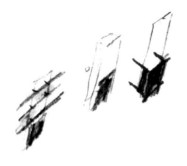

Fotografías: Jordi Miralles

On the facade of the building, the architect attempts to modify the image of such familiar elements as balconies and long windows.

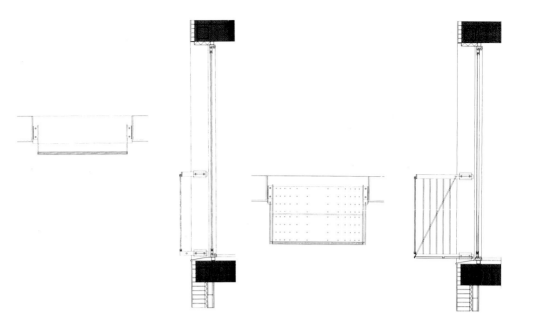

Construction detail of the window

Detail of the flooring on the balcony

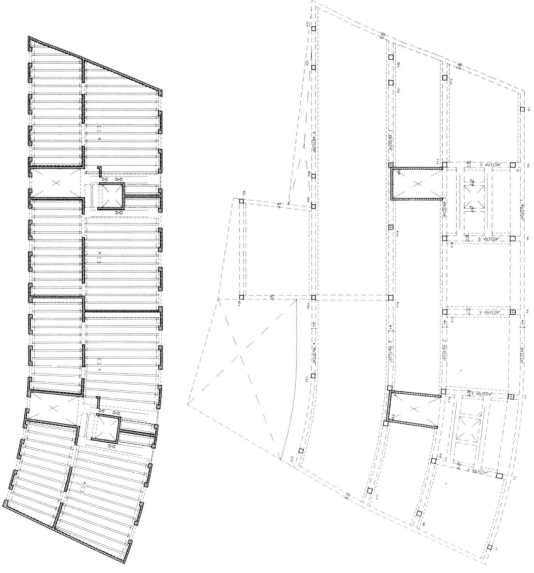

Structural plans

Structural plan of the floor framework

On the lower level, which is intended for public services, the building is perfectly adapted to the dimensions of the street. Different views of the main entrance and emergency exit are shown on this page.

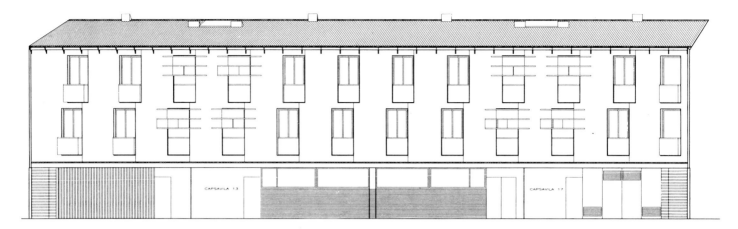

North elevation

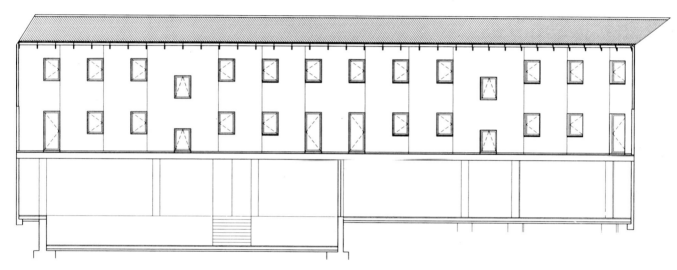

South-east elevation

Typical floor plan

The interplay of colour, texture and geometry is the dominant theme in the project. Sobriety and a skillful use of materials contribute to the reinterpretation of an old, well-defined typology.

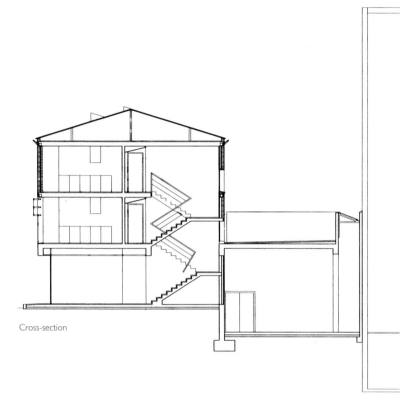

Cross-section

W.J. Neutelings

Two housing projects in Borneo Sporenburg and "de Hollainhof"

Amsterdam, The Netherlands / Ghent, Belgium

The apartments in Borneo Sporenburg, Amsterdam, form part of a master plan for the development of .the old jetties to the east of Amsterdam, an area characterised by long and narrow strips of land. The abandonment of port activity in this area has led to a gradual transformation of the district into a residential area. The project provides for 27 dwellings based on three different types of apartment, each with.its own entrance from the street and a private garden.

The distribution of the apartments facilitates the use of natural lighting, views and intimacy. The language formula chosen by the architects represents a deliberate allusion to the traditional architecture of the jetties that formerly occupied the site. All the facades are clad in hard industrial brick, combined on the ground floor with the metal of the handrails and grates and with cedar wood in the structure of roofs and terraces.

The project "De Hollainhof", in Ghent, consists of a social housing complex containing 120 apartments and an underground car park with a capacity for 90 cars. The aim of the scheme was to create an attractive habitat that combined the concepts of urbanity and density with those of tranquillity and privacy. The result is a complex that merges elements of both large and small scale.

The apartments are developed inside two large longitudinal volumes, one that skirts the street and one that runs along the river bank. These strips are composed of fifteen blocks, each one containing between eight and ten apartments. The area between the two volumes forms a large green area. From the city, the complex is reached through a long tunnel leading to the courtyard, from which the dwellings are accessed: each one has its own garden with an entrance from the common courtyard. Numerous recesses in the ground plan create a varied programme of room typologies within a set of cedar-clad geometries with a clear identity.

Photographs: Rob 'T Hart, Sara Blee

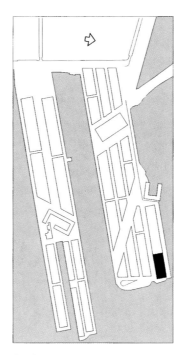

Site plan

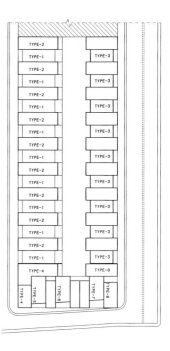

Housing typologies

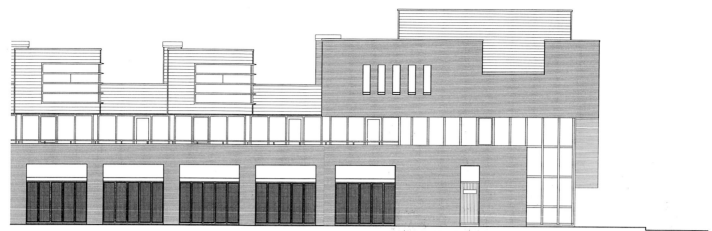

South elevation

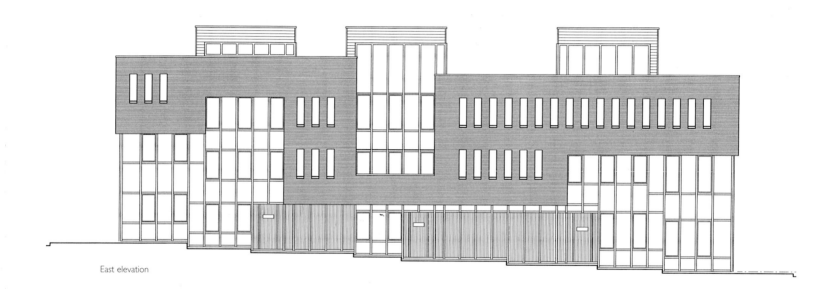

East elevation

North elevation

These dwellings were conceived as a spatial puzzle that is developed in both height and depth. Thus, each one enjoys light and views, its own entrance from the street, a garden and roof terraces. The lower part, clad in industrial ceramic tiles, is developed as a series of walls that are alternately open and closed. The upper part was clad with wooden slats of bevelled red cedar.

Cross sections

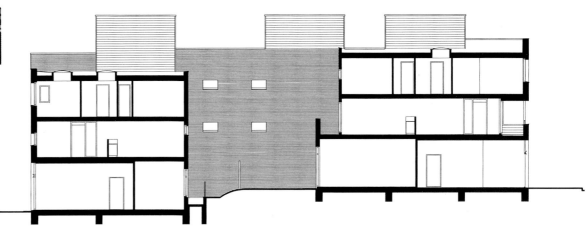

237

1. Entry
2. Hall
3. Garage
4. Carport
5. Storage
6. Study
7. Study
8. Garden room

Ground floor plan

17. Hall
18. Living room
19. Kitchen
20. Bedroom
21. Bathroom
22. Storage
23. Void
24. Terrace

Second floor plan

9. Hall
10. Living room
11. Kitchen
12. Bedroom
13. Bathroom
14. Winter garden
15. Terrace
16. Storage

First floor plan

25. Hall
26. Balcony
27. Void
28. Terrace

Upper level floor plan

239

Sporenburg and "de Hollainhof"

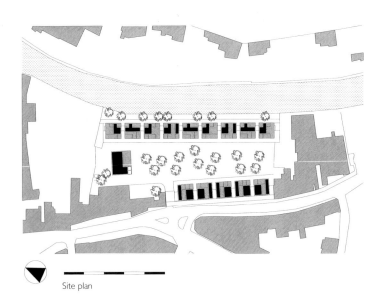

Site plan

The residential project has generated an extensive typological variety of dwellings which are laid out in a series of sculptural blocks with a clear identity.

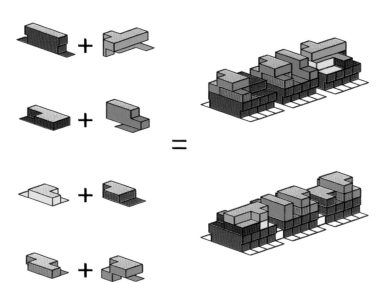

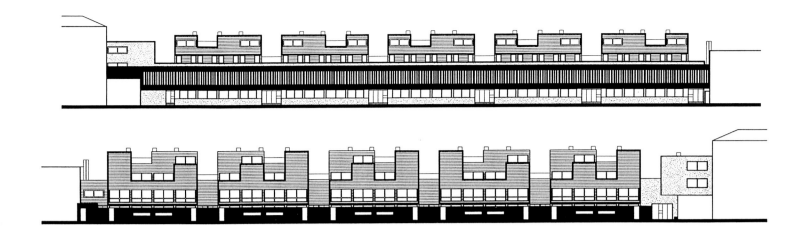

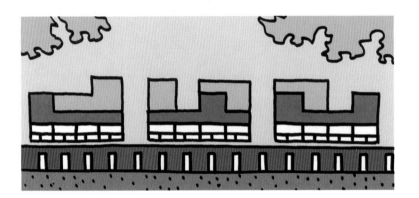

The cedar wood used in the upper part will gradually turn grey, contrasting with the terracotta colour of the prefabricated concrete walls that close the private courtyards.

Beat Consoni

Apartment House in Seestrasse

Horn, Switzerland

The project, an apartment house situated in the village centre of Horn, between the main street of the city and a public bathing area by the lake. The basement floor is developed inside an excavated rectangular space, with the particularity that it does not occupy this space entirely. The apartment block is thus perceived as a floating cube in opposition to the traditional concept of building over an underground basement that cannot be seen from the exterior. In this tub stands a core, which is reduced to slabs at basement level and creates a parking area.

In the upper floor, the core consists of the stairwell, the bathrooms and the kitchens of the individual apartments. The concrete slab of the ground floor is partly overhanging and supports the load of the upper floors. The structural concept of the core and the columns behind the facade allows flexible room divisions in the apartments. On the south side is a two-storey maisonette. This can be used individually or joined to one or the other apartment. Instead of single, individual balconies, the windows of the glass facade are constructed with sliding windows, opening the apartment towards the lake.

The apartments share a roof garden which can be accessed by the stairwell. This terrace can be divided into individual, private areas. The west facade has sliding blinds, protecting from heat and extreme weather conditions. The static and special concept creates a light, nearly hovering cube, in contrast to the traditional basement construction in this area.

Photographs: Michael Egloff + Markus Baumgartner

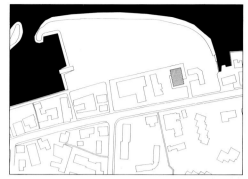

The basement floor is developed inside an excavated rectangular space, with the particularity that it does not occupy this space entirely. The apartments block is thus perceived as a floating cube in opposition to the traditional concept of building over an underground basement that cannot be seen from the exterior.

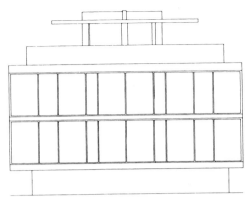

Side elevation

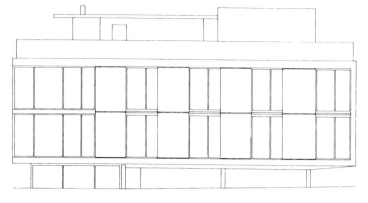

Main elevation

Cross-section

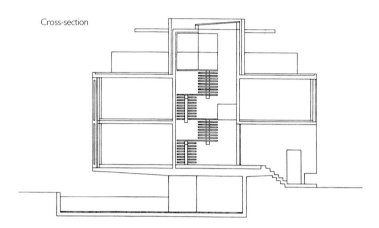

On both the outside and inside of the building there is a predominant use of exposed reinforced concrete and metal frames. These materials seem to glow thanks to the light flowing in from the skylight at the top of the staircase.

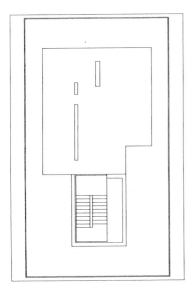

Roof terrace

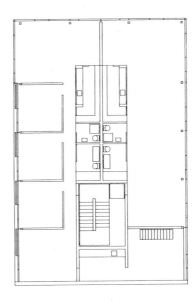

First floor plan

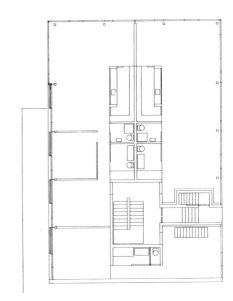

Ground floor plan

The structural layout, with service nuclei and load-bearing pillars located in a plane set back from the facade, provides total freedom for distributing the interiors and composing the facades.

The concrete floor slabs of the upper floors overhang the basement floor. The excavated area is used for parking, while on the upper floors this space houses the staircase and the bathrooms and kitchens of the individual apartments.

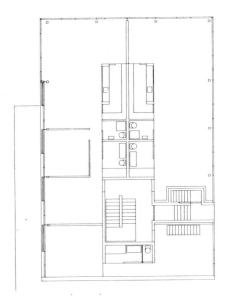

Basement floor plan

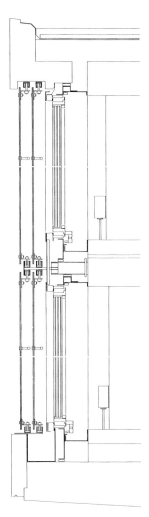

Construction section through the facade

On the south side, where the duplex-type dwelling is located, there are no balconies but sliding windows open the apartment toward the lake. The east facade is protected from the sunlight by sliding blinds.

Helin & Siitonen

Experimental House

Boras, Sweden

Living at the end of the 20th century calls for a new approach to planning new housing solutions, and new types of houses. This experimental house is formed by two wedges with an atrium between them, i.e. an extended stairwell forming a central common area. All apartments are entered through this area on the ground level, through the staircase and corridors, or using the private stairs directly to the second floor apartments. The connections with the existing human landscape and the verdant nature have served as a starting point in the design of this house. The same principle has been followed in the whole Hestra area, to minimise the changes in the landscape. The house includes 24 one-level apartments on the top floor sized 63 sqm. (8 rooms + kitchen) and eight of them of 97 sqm. (4 rooms + kitchen). These two-level apartments have a sauna and terrace on the roof. The foyer and the kitchen are located along the atrium, but the bedrooms and the living room are along the more private and quiet outer side of the wedge. The apartments are flexible, highly functional in a variety of living conditions and well sui ted to different lifestyles. The framework of the building is reinforced concrete. To emphasise the connection with nature this building has a turf roof. All vertical installations, air conditioning, plumbing and electrical, are assembled on the facades around the atrium, making them accessible for service and changes.

Photographs: Tita Lumio

Site plan

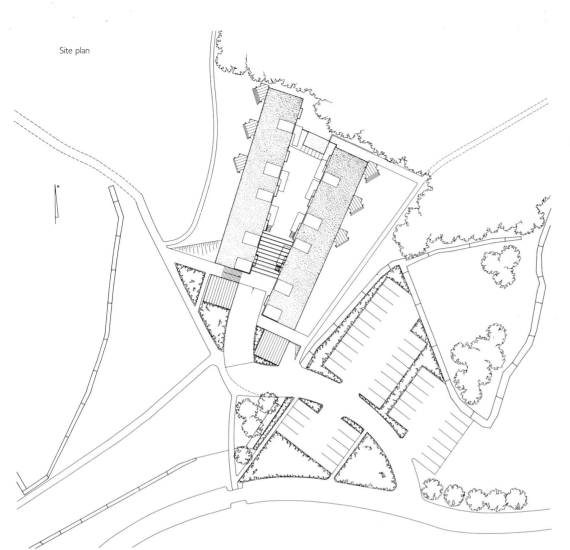

The water insulation is covered by a 20 cm thick layer of sods overlaid with soil and seeded; the future development of the greenery will be the work of nature.

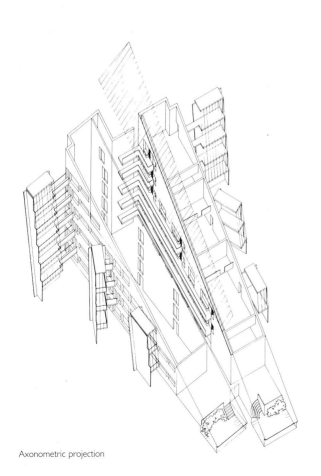

Axonometric projection

249

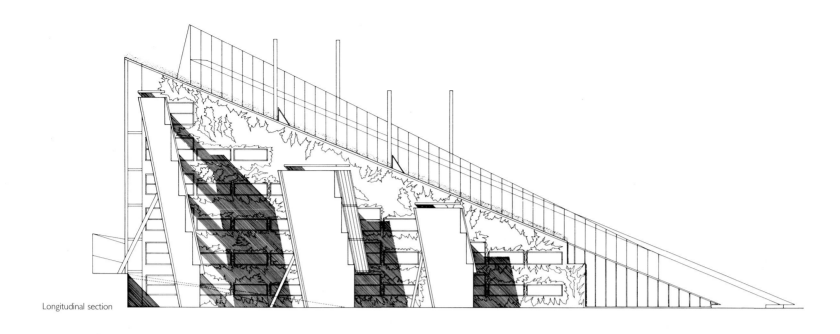

Longitudinal section

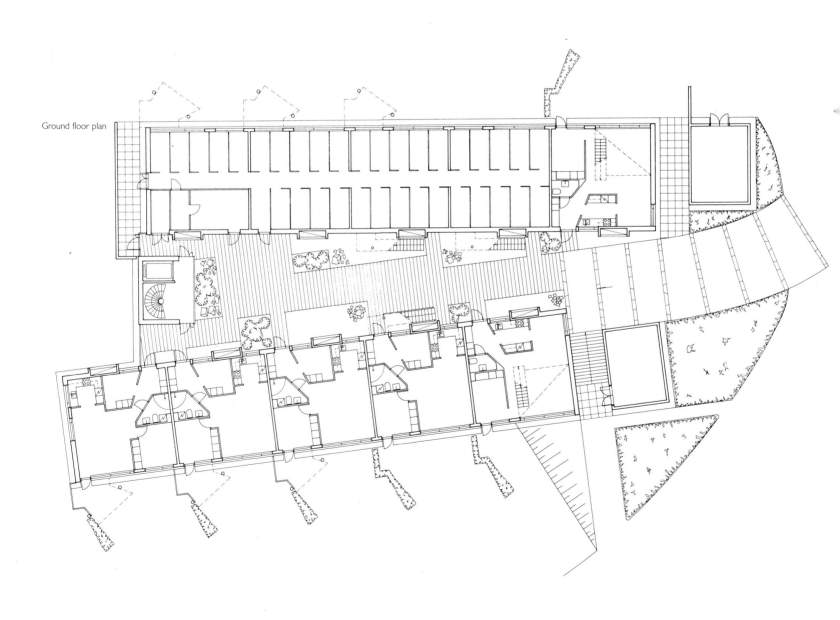

Ground floor plan

Second floor plan

Upper level floor plan

0 1 2   5   10

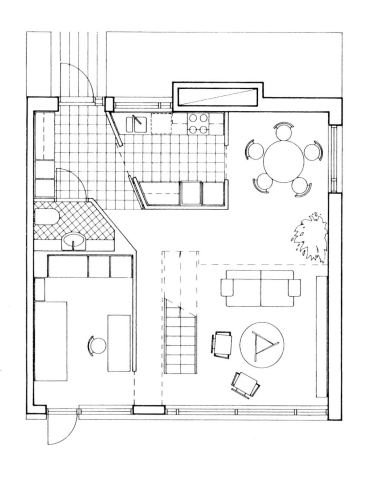

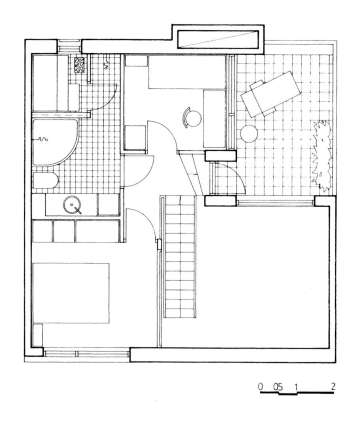

0 05 1 2

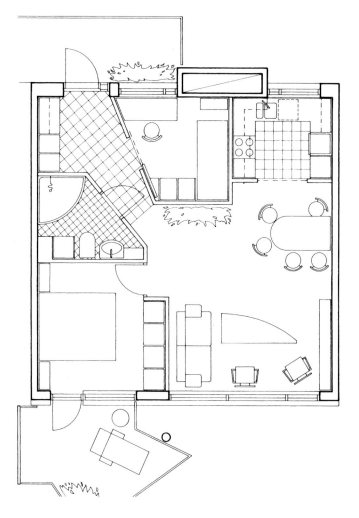

STANDARD LEVELS
All these apartments have penetration to two different directions, which makes them spacious and well lighted. This impression is emphasised by the long diagonal views from the entrance, through the living room to the surrounding nature.

Santiago Calatrava

Buchen Housing Estate

Würenlingen, Suiza

Coexisting with other developments in an open landscape, this series of homes is positioned parallel to the main road of the small town of Würlingen, close to Zürich. The project called for the construction of twenty-four free-standing dwellings to be arranged in two twelve-unit rows flanking a square, and three groups of six terraced houses to the south of the site, right at the edge of a wooded area. The client, Remer Real Estate, specified concrete to be the main material used in the entire colony, for which reason all the external facades are constructed with prefabricated concrete elements. The shape of the building –with the top floor having a wider floor area than the lower ones– is on account of restrictive conditions of the site. The land drops down slightly from the woods, and the slope is used to lock the section and create a series of exterior spaces at different levels. On the low northern side the ground floor opens on to the spa-

cious main entrance portico, while on the other side, staircases –one for each successive pair of units– connect the back doors to the wood's raised land. The backyards on this level are stepped onto straight from the living rooms, which stretch from front to rear.

The rooms of a more public nature look out to the double-height portico, creating a semi-glazed facade. Only a narrow concrete panel separates one volume from the other. The volume containing the top floor bedrooms –a total of three per unit– begins right above this continuous and communal arcade space to stretch back toward the woods under a shell-shaped roof.

The forward projection of the upper floor is accentuated by the windows of the front bedrooms, which look like eyes staring vacantly at the landscape. A stylised pillar situated at the transversal axis of each dwelling sustains the load of the top floor obliquely, and gives the complex its characteristic image.

Fotografías: Hans Ege

256

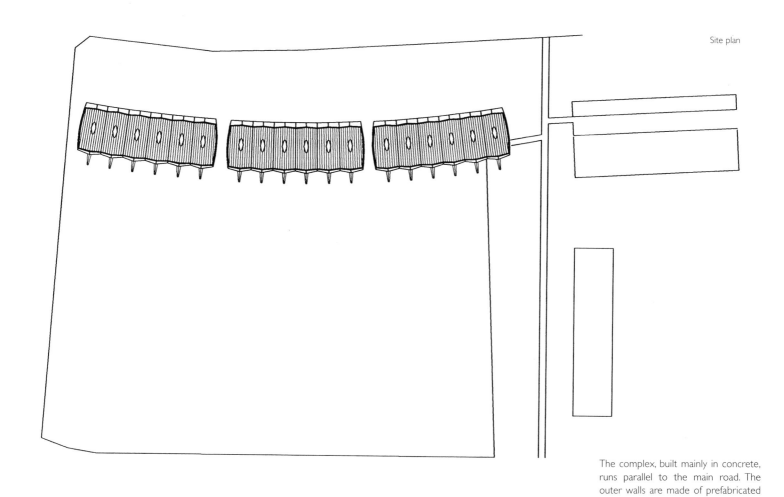

The complex, built mainly in concrete, runs parallel to the main road. The outer walls are made of prefabricated concrete elements.

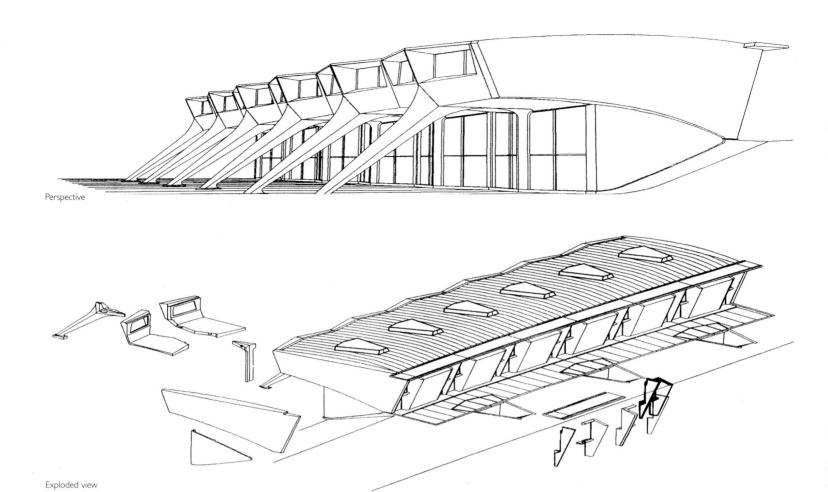

Perspective

Exploded view

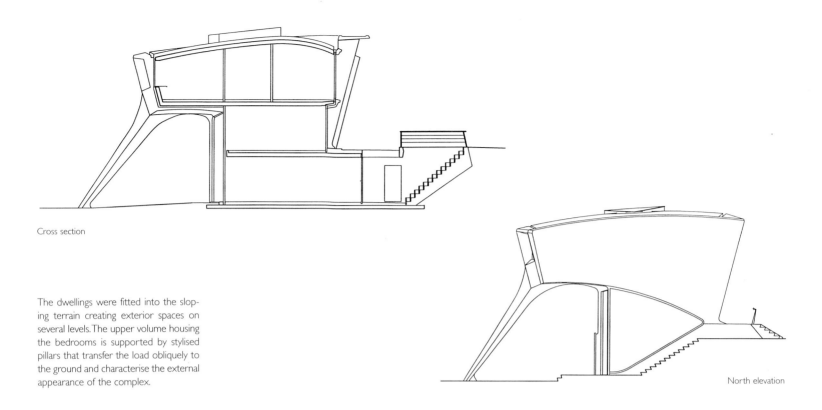

Cross section

The dwellings were fitted into the sloping terrain creating exterior spaces on several levels. The upper volume housing the bedrooms is supported by stylised pillars that transfer the load obliquely to the ground and characterise the external appearance of the complex.

North elevation

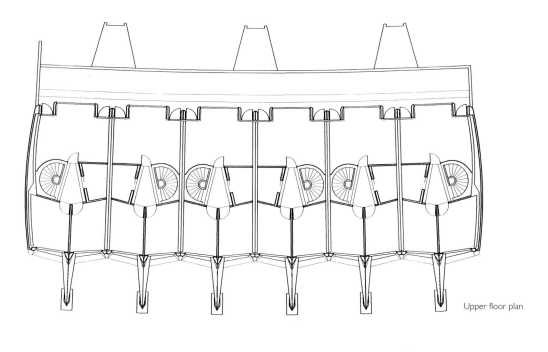

Upper floor plan

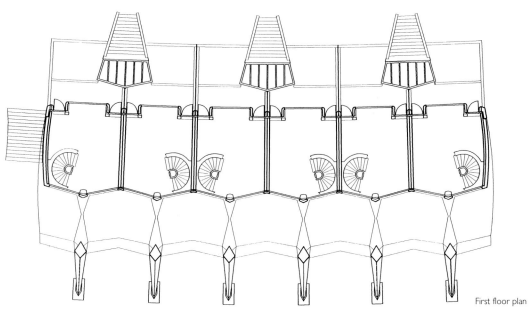

First floor plan

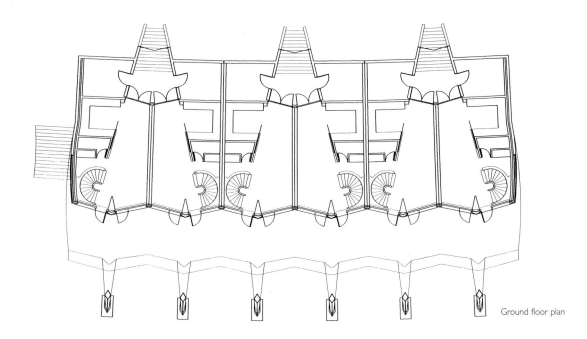

Ground floor plan

261

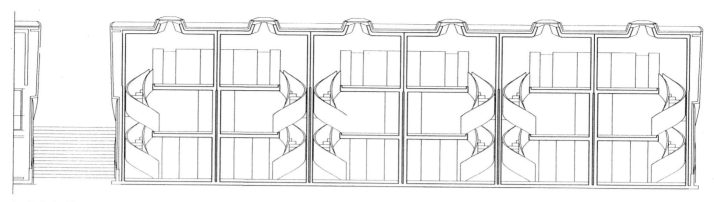

Longitudinal section

The more public premises open onto
the double-height portico that is common to all the dwellings. Above this
space the upper volumes of the
dwellings protrude, separated only by
small screens.

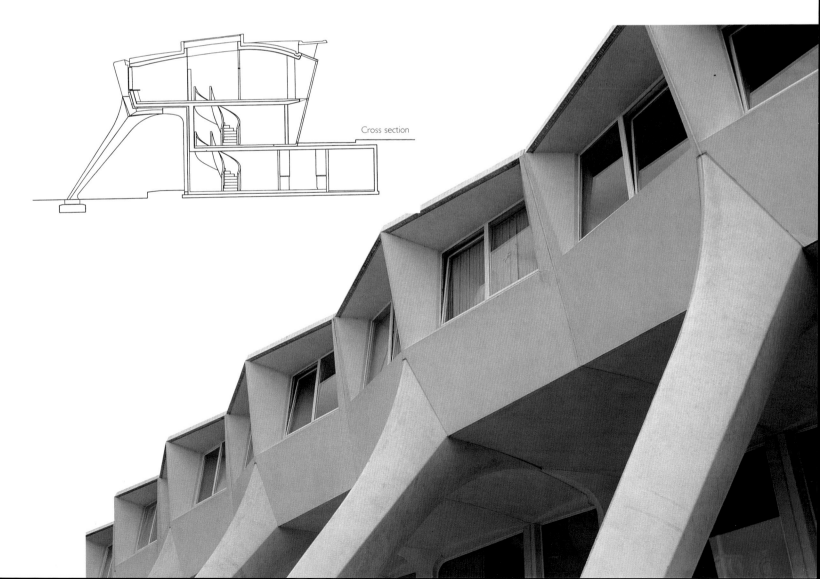

Cross section

Manfred Wolff-Plottegg

Wohnbebaung Seiersberg

Seiersberg, Austria

Faced with one block, that is still a fragment of the residential settlement, one is clearly reminded of over one hundred years of tradition of Styran workers homes. However, historicism was certainly not on Wolff-Plottegg's mind. The old type of houses with access balconies of the ore, iron and coal regions with their small private rooms and their oversized connecting common areas have here entered into a kind of ingenious synthesis with the ever changing values of the modern residential block. The old features are therefore not part of convention, but only of the handling of convention. Plottegg designed a type of house with two flats per floor. The privatised outside zone –the balconies– is oriented towards the south and the development passes through this zone. Thus, the architect does not only destroy the hermetics of "front" and "back", he also entwines private and common spaces and creates a communication area. In addition, the common "action area" made up of compartments becomes a sort of multi-storey "simultaneous stage" due to the huge braced girder of the suspension of the balcony. The main characteristic of the flats is their individual permeability. The floor-to-ceiling windows and doors provide the spatial sparingness with a certain noblesse. In addition, the most important rooms are trapezoidal, since the eye always perceives the larger dimensions. A similar trick makes the zone of the balconies wider; the continuous braced girder angles slightly away from the facade so that the actual room is slightly detached from the visual one.

The rear of the building, a transparent striped facade becomes "out of scale" as it obscures its length and height in favour of the large form, thus forming a dialogue with the dimensions of the context's architecture.

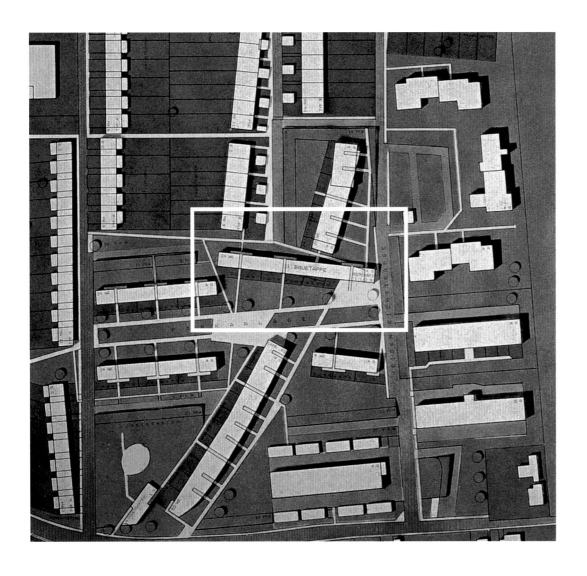

The scheme of the Seiersberg project arises from the redevelopment of an area of low density development located on the outskirts of the Swiss city of Graz. The architect Manfred Wolff-Plottegg tried to break with the classic model of suburban buildings, creating a very sunny architecture and enjoying a high degree of privacy regarding the interiors.

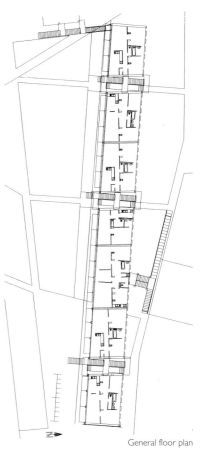

General floor plan

265

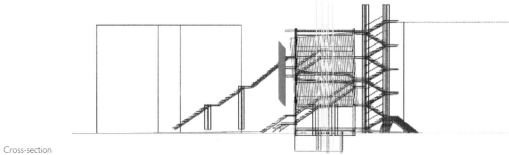

Cross-section

Large glazed floor-to-ceiling openings increase the dimensions of the rooms visually. This effect is increased by a trapezoidal ground plan. The transparency and generosity of the apartments guarantee spatial width and flexibility. The building can be used well without compromising its architecture.

The blocks were arranged longitudinally. A central axis and the location of the kitchen and bathrooms structure the layout of the interior of the dwellings.

Typical plan of the apartments

1. Entrance
2. Kitchen
3. Living-room
4. Bedroom
5. Main bedroom
6. Bathroom
7. Toilet
8. Shower

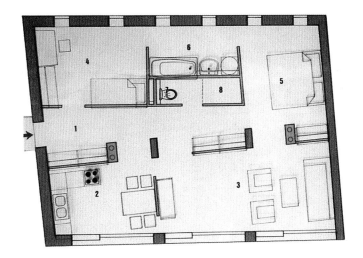

Khun Fischer

Leimatt

Oberwil-Zug, Switzerland

Due to the new economic circumstances there is once more a market for economy housing. This project forms part of a group of seven in which Kuhn Fischer & Partner have created economical accommodation through the skillful use of zoning and construction.

Swiss pragmatism is the keynote. Conventional local building techniques are used, and small defects are allowed. Cheaper materials and few elements are used in response to the question: what is really needed?

But economy also leads to an astonishing flexibility of design and use. All the walls are straight and rise vertically through all floors. Each room has the same width, so when halved, special entrances, bathrooms and internal halls can be created. Two room widths provide a range of possibilities.

It is possible to change the arrangement of the individual apartment sizes during the design and building stage, and to adapt the space of each apartment during use. Both types of flexibility are reached by the same means: using "switchrooms", "separation rooms" and the corridor zones as free intermediate axes. Switch rooms can be added to the left or right apartment through the modification of the layout of the doors and corridor ends. Separation rooms are always near to the second bathroom of a large apartment. Thus, through the incorporation of a small kitchen a small flat can be separated from the main one.

Each apartment has a front and a back. The front is the entrance and the rear the garden facade. At the front is a semi-private entrance walkway and at the back a private balcony.

Kuhn Fischer & Partner use accumulation as a solution to the building of apartments. They show that much can be learned from the past at a time when little new remains to be discovered.

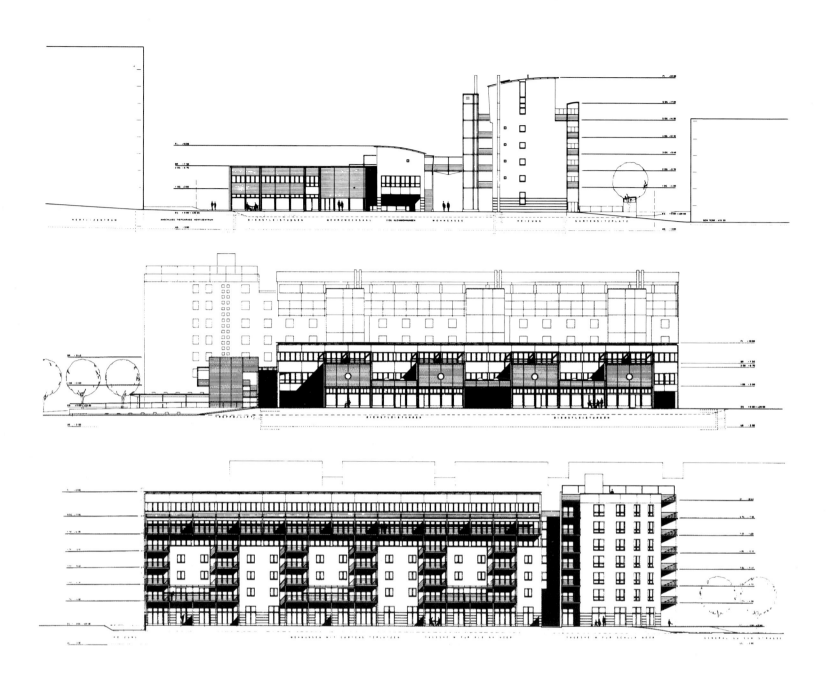

Cross section

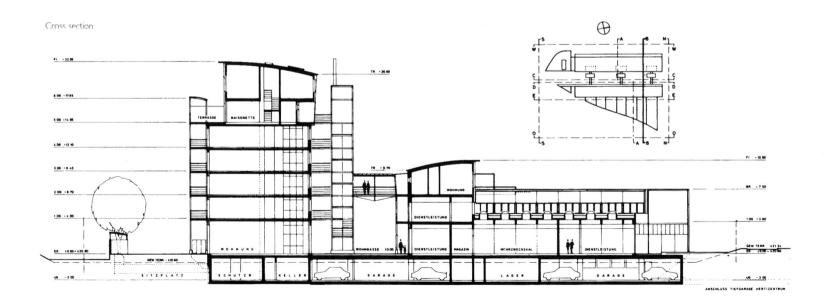

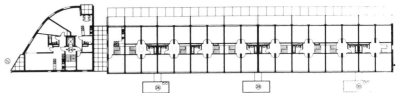

Second floor plan

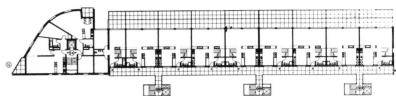

Upper level floor plan

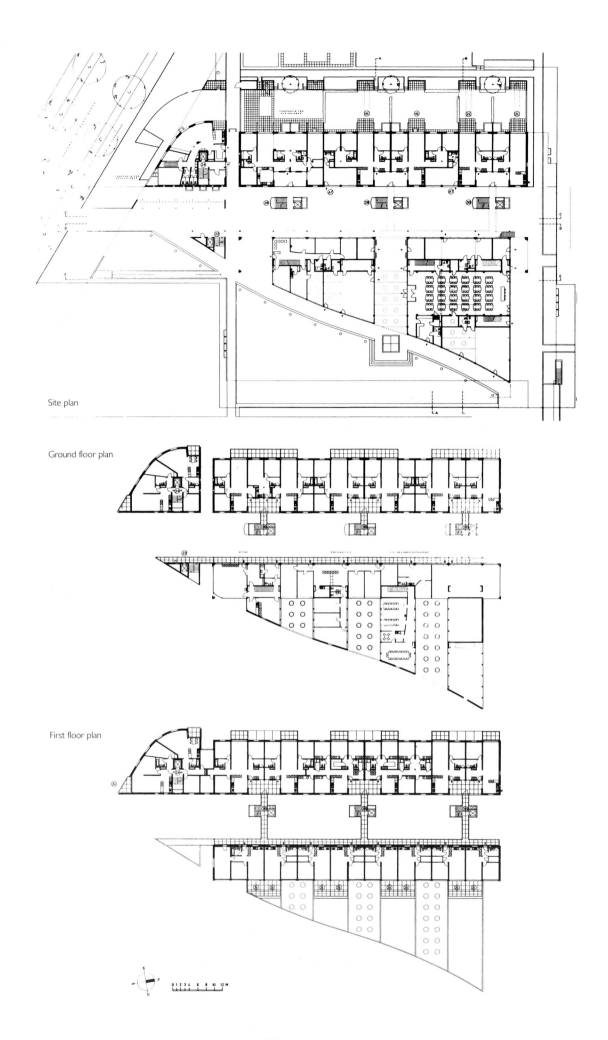

Site plan

Ground floor plan

First floor plan

274

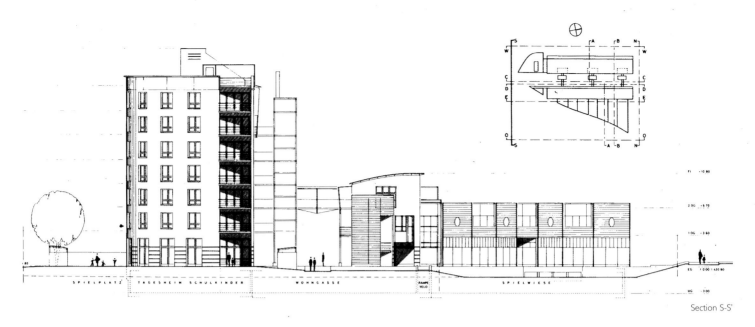

Section S-S'

The building is characterised by the use of few architectural elements, cheap materials and local building techniques. View of the private balcony on the facade overlooking the garden.

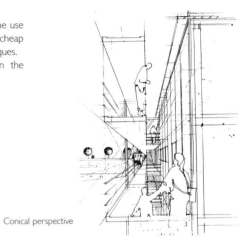

Conical perspective

Frank O. Gehry
Goldstein Sud Housing Development
Frankfurt, Germany

The project is located approximately 8 kilometres of downtown Frankfurt at the eastern edge of a public housing zone known as Goldstein South. The site is the last undeveloped public housing track in the area and provides connections to a community sports field, a future tram stop and educational facilities. The program comprises a semi-public park and 162 units of housing with related parking areas, a social centre and neighbourhood retail. The project distributes the park along the natural circulation paths for use by the community. The North/South axis connects the Goldenstein Park with the Greenbelt, while the East/West axis connects the Goldstein South housing with the future tram stop and educational facilities thereby serving these daily needs. The two paths are recognisable by distinct types of landscape materials: the north/South path is planted with a variety of trees to create a natural setting connecting the park and the Greenbelt.

On the other side, the East/West transportation path is organised within a linear grid of flowering trees with hardscape paths that accomodate frequent bicycle travel.

The apartment blocks are organised in a manner that creates partially enclosed courtyards. These courtyards are further divided by paths, terraces and private gardens to provide a variety of spaces.

The internal plans of the housing units vary according to their disposition relative to site amenities and orientation. Three basic strategies yield a variety of plan typologies. The units that are linear along the East/West axis have south exposure for living, dining and kitchen areas yielding sunshine and views to the Greenbelt. The units that are linear along the North/South axis have the living, dining and kitchen areas oriented perpendicular to the length of the building. This allows these living zones to have both morning and afternoon sunshine.

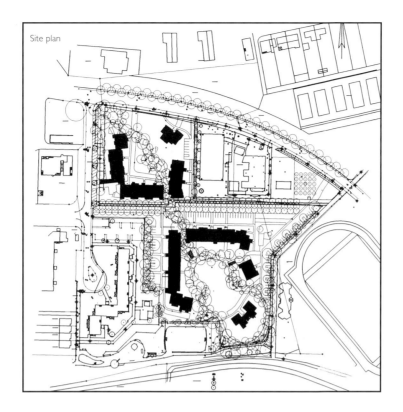

Site plan

The programme includes the creation of a large semi-public park. The solution adopted by the architect locates the park as an integral part of the natural circulation routes used by the new community. The dwelling blocks have been located so that they emphasise these routes.

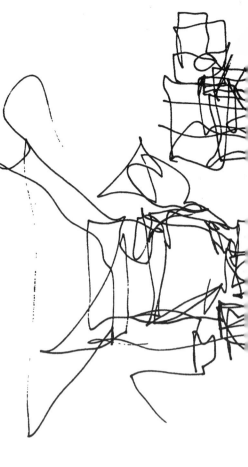

The building aesthetic is derived through the building forms that emphasise entries, stairs, penthouses and balconies. These forms are emphasised with zinc panels while boldly coloured plaster facades comprise the major surface material.

The interior organisation is exposed on the exterior through the use of zinc panels that clad and formally highlight certain parts of the building: entrance lobbies, staircase nuclei, balconies and lofts.

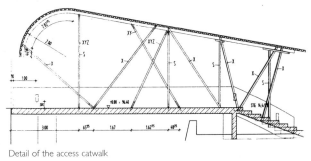

Detail of the access catwalk

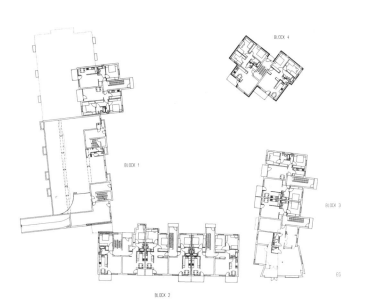

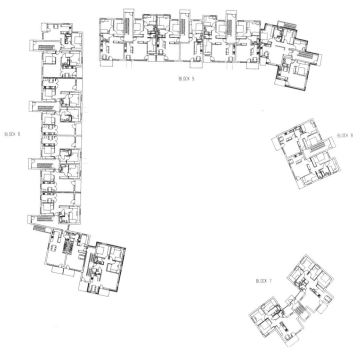

The colour, texture and rotundity of shapes and volumes of the areas done in sheets of zinc contrasts with the level planes and formal simplicity of the rest of the surfaces comprising the various facades of this residential complex.

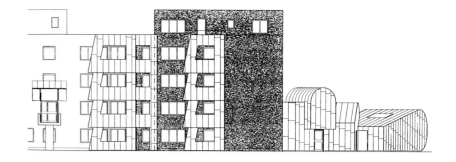

With views of the park, the rows of dwellings have been built with the traditional construction method of rendered masonry walls, painted in colours ranging from white to earth to ochre.

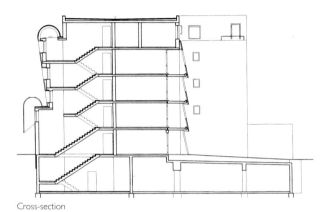

Cross-section

Architectuur studio Herman Hertzberger
Housing Complex
Düren, Germany

The building, by the firm of the Dutch architect Herman Hertzberger, is located in a rather dismal part of the German town of Düren. Instead of keeping to the prescribed extension plan and distributing the building blocks all over the site, the project arranges them in a line along the perimeter of the site, thus creating a square building block around a green court in the interior.

This court is accessible from all sides and a street runs over it in the middle, so access to the dwellings is through this community space.

The major presence of the continuous roof and the plinth, which shows the difference in building height, provides the whole with a close and clearly defined form.

At the same time, these two elements unify the whole complex. All dwellings have their entry on the court side and, depending on the housing typology, can be reached directly by stairs or over the different galleries.

Photographs: Jens Willebrand

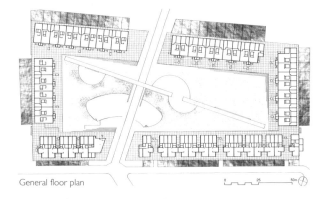

General floor plan

0   25   50m

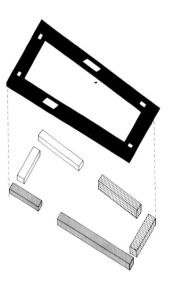

The architect has organised the complex in the form of a linear block distributed along the perimeter of the site, so that it rotates around a green area located in the interior. The access to the dwellings is through this community space.

Sketch

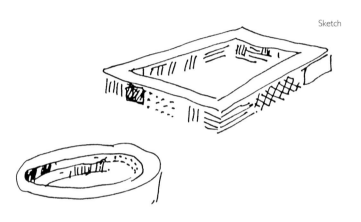

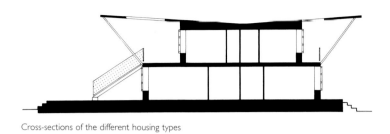

Cross-sections of the different housing types

As can be seen in the photograph below, the four streets that define the site give access to the interior space.

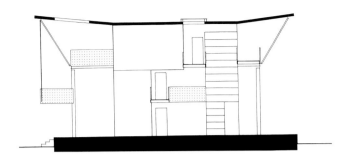

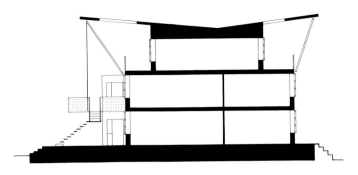

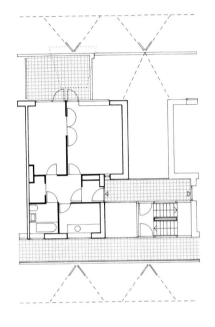

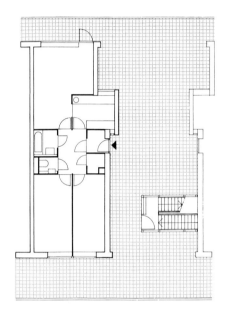

C-TYPE DWELLING

Ground and first floor plans

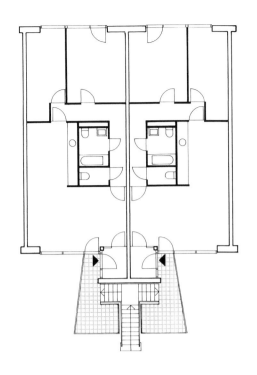
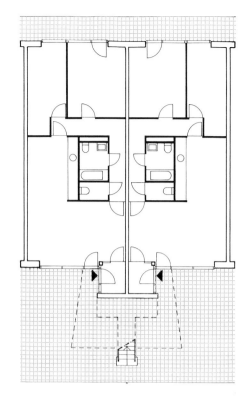

B-TYPE DWELLING

Ground and first floor plans

Annette Gigon & Mike Guyer

Residential complex in Kilchberg

Kilchberg, Switzerland

The land around the Broëlberg residence, an early 20th century villa, consists of a park bordering on open landscape, near Zürich Lake.

In this green area, that now is in great demand from the people who prefer to reside outside the urban environs, it was planned to build a residential complex selecting six sites with concentrated, volumetrically distinct three-storey buildings with varying concepts of habitation. Three buildings by the architectural team Gigon & Guyer are the only ones finished until now. They form a volumetric complex linked via a one-storey podium with space for parking underneath. The podium itself forms a raised courtyard which provides access to the buildings.

Two of the buildings house four apartments and a penthouse each, the third consists of a row of four units. In most of the apartments, the kitchen and dining areas face the podium while the living room with projecting conservatory and the bedrooms face the landscape. The

podium itself, a large surface of poured concrete slabs, glass brick and gravel is subdivided into a public access area and semiprivate outdoor seating by means of pavilion-shaped steel structures with plywood planking.

Large windows, like huge eyes, offer a magnificent view of the lake and the surrounding park. A broad aluminium frame somewhat like a cornice encases the blinds, guide rails and wooden window frames. The free-style arrangement of the floor-to-ceiling openings responds to the different types of apartments.

The main facades are masonry with exterior insulation and a fine, evenly coloured, stucco that encases the building like a smooth skin.

The dark brown colour of the outside walls is juxtaposed with the light orange walls of the courtyard, generating intense colouring in this space that varies with changes in the natural lighting during the day.

Site plan

The brown colour chosen for the external facades ennobles the structure of the building and establishes a close relationship with its soft organic composition.

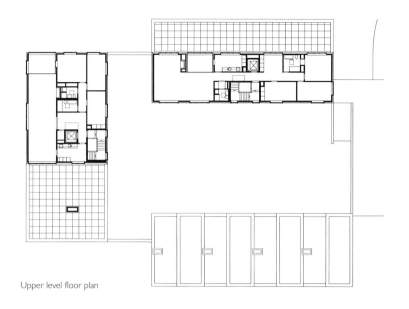

Upper level floor plan

Second floor plan

First floor plan

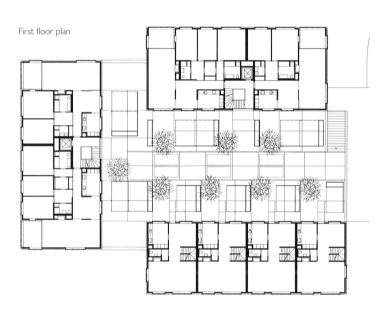

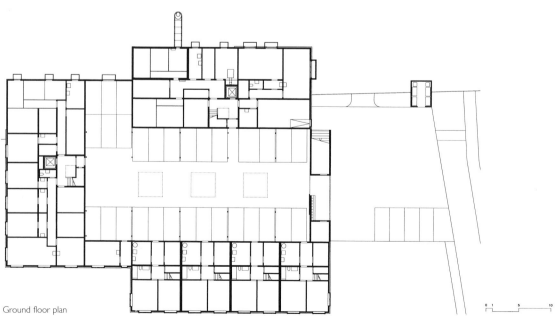

Ground floor plan

0 1   5   10

The inner courtyard is organised by means of semi-public spaces in front of the dwellings built with a metal frame and plywood boards.

In the photographs below we can see the strong contrast between the dark brown colour of the east facade and the orange colour of the facades that look onto the inner courtyard.

West elevation

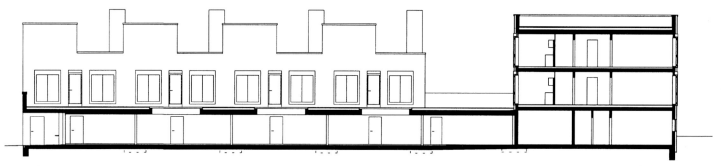

North-south section

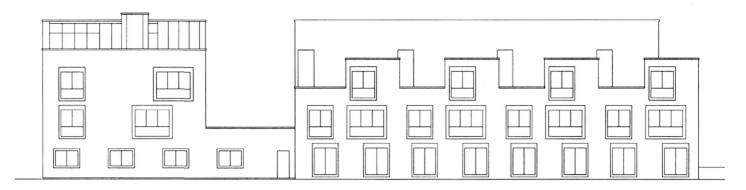

East elevation

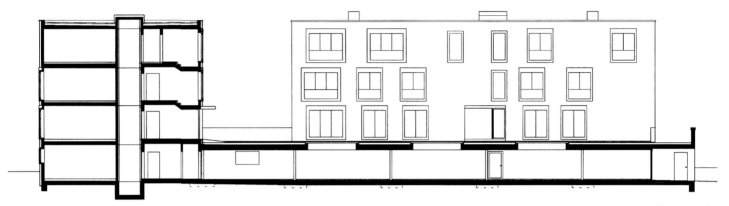

East-west section

Large glazed openings spanned between wrought iron workings allow a constant and uninterrupted relation between the interior and exterior of the dwellings. Thus, wide views of the park surrounding the residential complex may be obtained.

Deubzer König Architects

Housing Project in Regensburg

Regensburg, Germany

The need to form a new place with urban qualities in this environment was essential. Considering the requirements of the building type (housing with a large number of equally oriented apartments) an orthogonal grid of L-shaped buildings was developed with south and west oriented apartments. The access corridors on the north and east facades and the vertical circulation cores in the corners are naturally lit. This grid is superimposed by the diagonal path, which leads to a certain distortion within the rectangular system. The enclosure of the courtyards is contrasted by dynamic views along this diagonal axis, which still serves as a public pathway through the site. Several modifications were necessary to adjust the scheme to the varying needs and budgets of two different clients. Student housing for the "Protestantische Alumneumsstiftung Regensburg" with rooms for 456 students, with an average of 18 m² per student, had to be built within a

very tight budget. The rooms are distributed among units of different sizes, from studio-apartments to 6-room flats. Each unit has a cooking facility and a bathroom.

Housing for employees of the medical faculty of the University of Regensburg with 180 studio-apartments (28 sqm per person) with bathroom and kitchen area. These were made within a comparatively tight budget.

According to these different requirements the two types vary in depth and axial spacing, materials and equipment. The student housing has a communal balcony-zone, serving as interactive community space. The employee housing has individual balconies providing a higher degree of privacy. The balconies facing the courtyards serve as shades for the apartments. As the bathroom and kitchen units are either round or reduced in height, a transparency is created within and through the apartments.

Photographs: Ulrich Schwarz

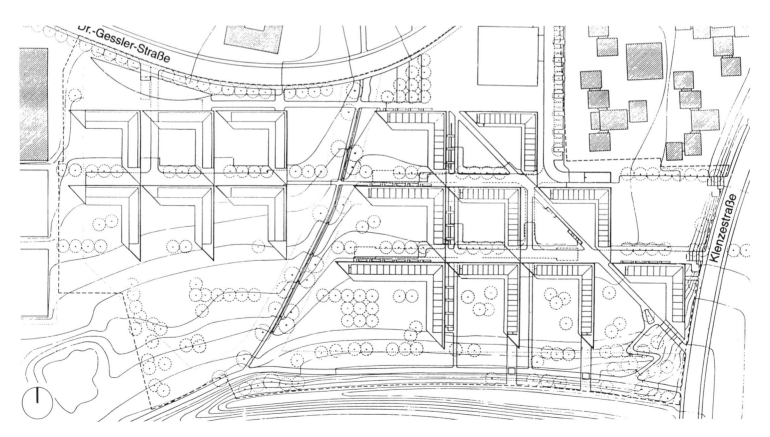

The intention was not to build a group of single buildings but an entity. This led to the use of unifying formal means: the intense red colour of the facade (mineral pigments of the same colour as old houses in the city), the connecting roof structures between the parts and the same absolute height of all roofs and eaves. Progressing down, the buildings seem to "grow" out of the hill.

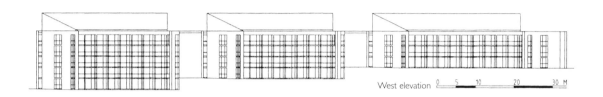

West elevation 0 5 10 20 30 M

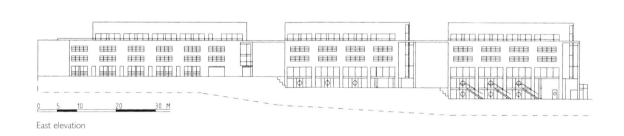

0 5 10 20 30 M

East elevation

Standard floor plan

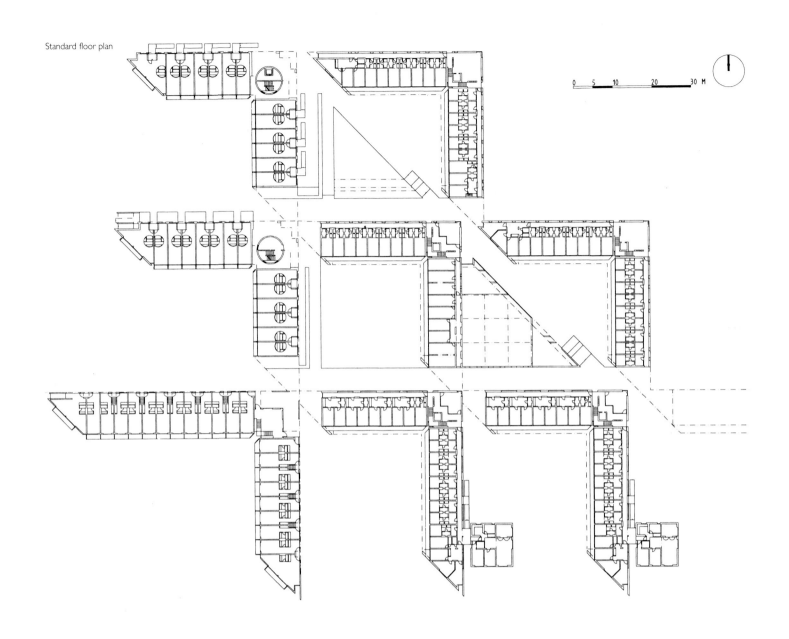

0 5 10   20   30 M

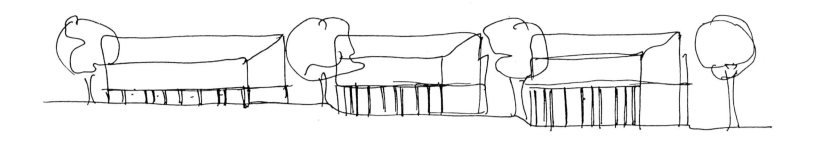

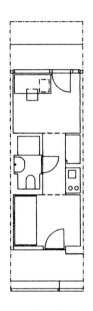

Type 1

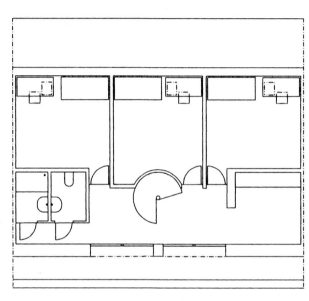

Upper level

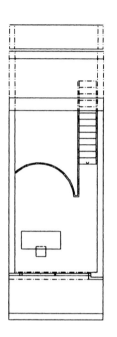

Upper level

Type 2

Lower level

Lower level

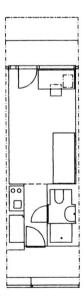

Student housing. Single-room apartments

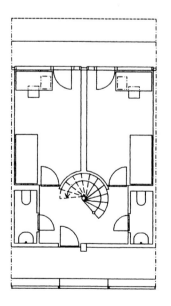

Student housing. Maisonette

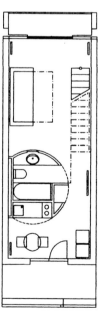

Nurses housing. Maisonette

The rooms have been distributed into units of different sizes, which go from studio-apartments to flats with up to six bedrooms. Each unit has its own kitchen and services. The different apartments have been adapted to the requirements and needs of the users, who are mostly students and employees of the faculty of medicine.

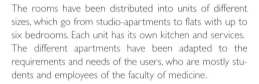

W.J. Neutelings Architectuur

Apartment Complex "Prinsenhoek"

Sittard, Netherlands

The "Prinsenhoek" project, situated on one of the most important crossroads of the Sittard city-centre, consists of three elements grouped around an inner garden: a 19th century villa, an apartment block and a car park.

The old villa, which would have been destroyed under the old city ordinance has been kept as an attractive historical element in the complex, and has been restored as offices. The gardens of the villa are used as a binding element in the whole plan, a quiet oasis in the city. The entrances, bay windows, gates and underpasses are finished in robust Ardennes flagstones, forming a plinth of urban fabric.

The three middle floors consist of a strong rectangular volume. This volume has a rhythm of deeply set windows cut out from its anthracite grey concrete facade. The roofline is described by a sculptural play of cedar-clad volumes, whose corners and setbacks form deluxe terraces from which the occupiers can observe the panoramic view of the Sittard city-centre. The courtyard gardens are situated at 1.5 metres beneath street level. This height difference means that the offices, which sit upon a layer of storage space at the garden level, acquire a measure of privacy as they are lifted high up above pedestrian view. This level change puts the old villa also on a podium when seen from within the garden.

All four entrance halls and stairwells to the apartments are reached from the garden side of the building via a ramped tunnel, gated on the street side, through the block. The high car park wall, on the other side of the site, cuts off the gardens from the hubbub of urban life.

Photographs: Kim Zwarts

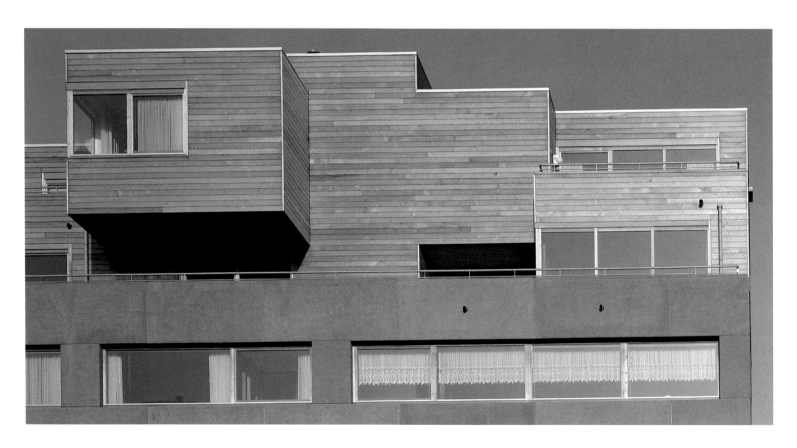

303

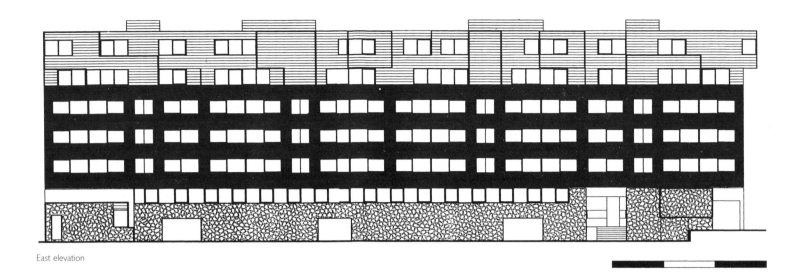

East elevation

5   10   15

Elevation and view of the north sector, with the nineteenth-century villa and the new structure of the building. On the following page: Elevation and view of the west facade.

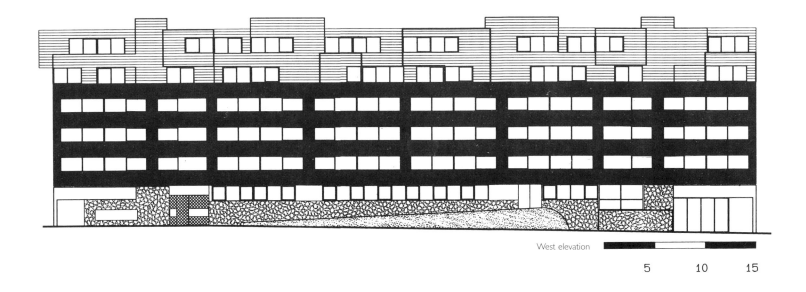

West elevation

5   10   15

The line of the roof is solved through a sculptural interplay of cedar-clad volumes, whose corners and inverted spaces form impressive terraces.

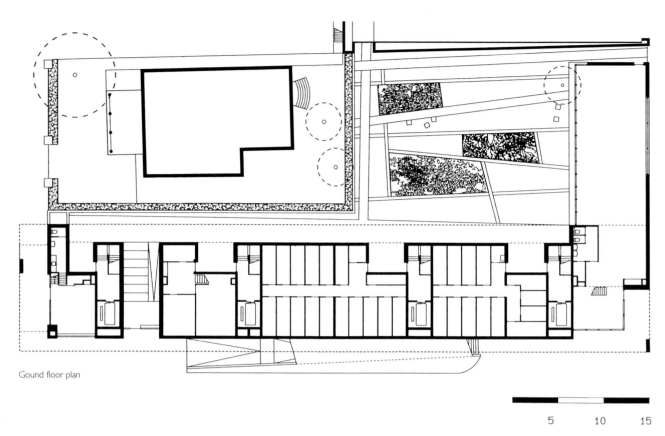

Gound floor plan

5   10   15

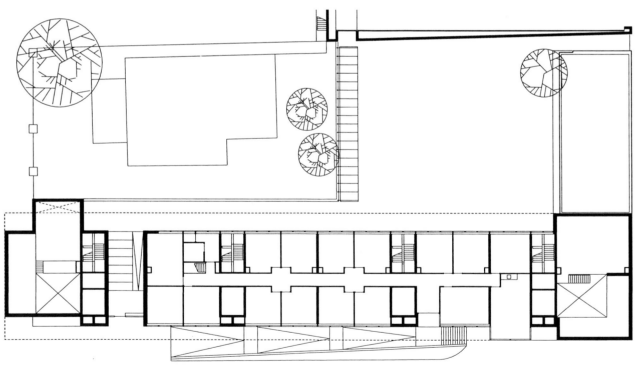

First floor plan

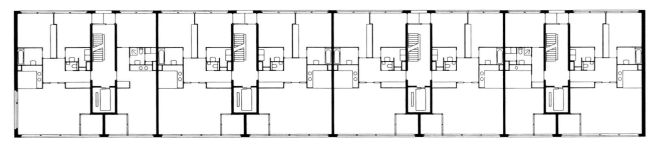

Second and third floor plan

Fourth floor plan

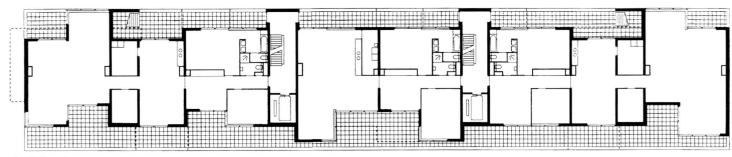

Upper level floor plan

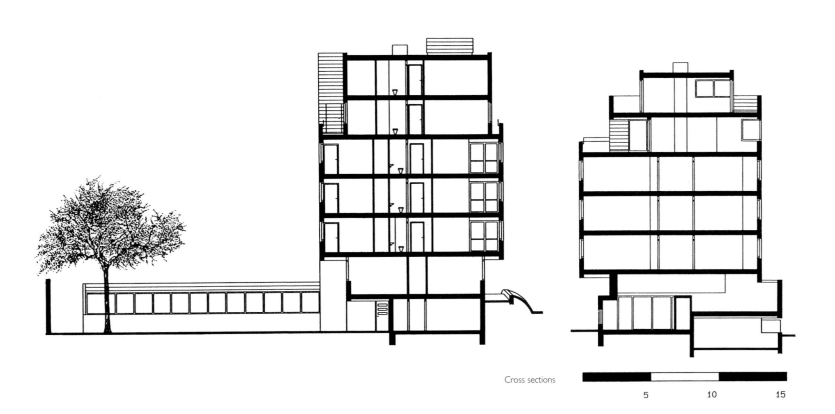

Cross sections

5   10   15

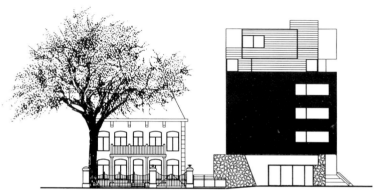

North elevation

On the upper levels, the cedar cladding serves to visually soften the singular volumetric interplays of the top floor, which is articulated as six villas.

The plinth that runs around the lower part of the complex naturally absorbs functional elements of great importance. Its visual strength also unifies the different elements of the dwelling.

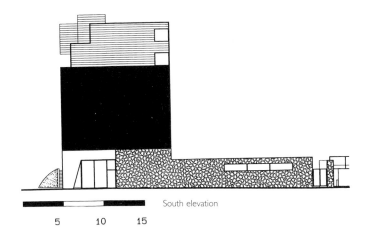

South elevation

5   10   15

Claus & Kaan

Ladsteinerlaan Housing

Groningen, The Netherlands

The Landsteinerlaan project is an urban infill in the *Corpus den Hoorn* district of Groningen. When the home for the elderly was demolished, an immense gap was left in the heart of the north-west Corpus quadrant. This building, in conjunction with the church, had previously formed the centre of the urban design. Any new housing should confirm the public nature of the site and keep the district's design idiom. It should link up, in dimensions, scale and typology, with the existing structure and expose and enhance the quality already present. The church is pivotal to the land division and anchors the design in its context.

The building volumes enclose the public green area while leaving the original open design structure of the district intact. The facades are abstract to void privatisation of the public character in any way. The spaces in between the head elevations of the apartment buildings and the alleys between the patio dwellings give access to the dwellings as well as to the public area. With regard to the landscaping, the main aim of the architects was to achieve maximum effect while minimising the sense of design.

Standard materials were used for paving, street lighting, plants and furniture. Their design and use reflect the character of the space adjoining the building volume. This is abstract on the side of the public garden and specific on that of the access areas.

The public lighting forms an integral part of the design. The existing lamp standards in the Landsteinerlaan have been removed and the street is now lit by the strip-lighting along the galleries which link up to form lines evoking a bar code.

The paving of the entire area is based on the use of 50x50 cm concrete paving slabs. The parallel development of the design and the layout made it possible for the measurements of the building blocks to be based on the size of the paving slabs. While this attention to detail does not stand out, its impact is clearly felt.

Photographs: Ger Van der Vlught

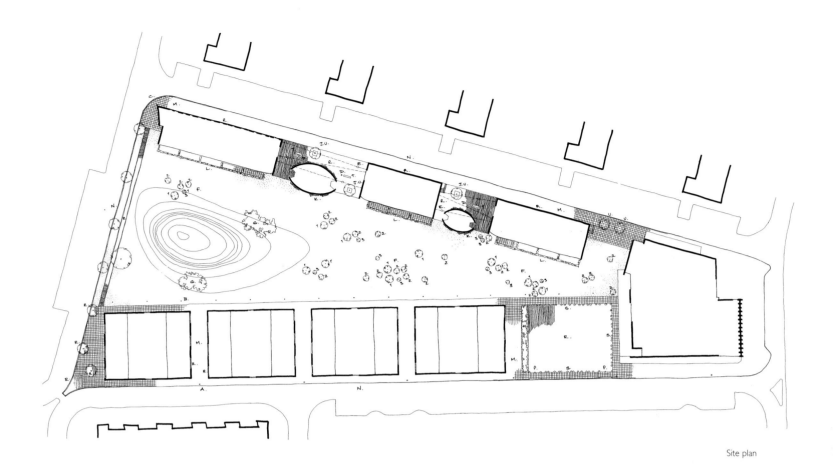

Site plan

The glazed galleries that give access to the dwellings facilitate and temper the transition between public and private spaces.

On this page, views of the public access area located in the interstitial spaces formed between the blocks of dwellings.

Previous sketch

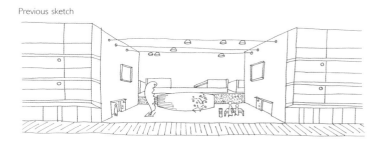

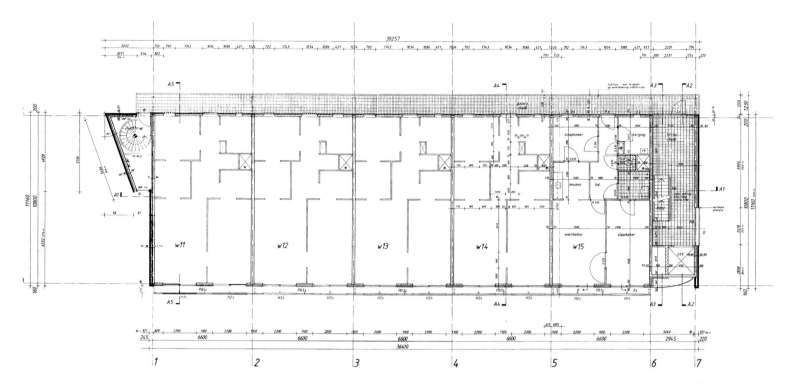

Floor plan of A block

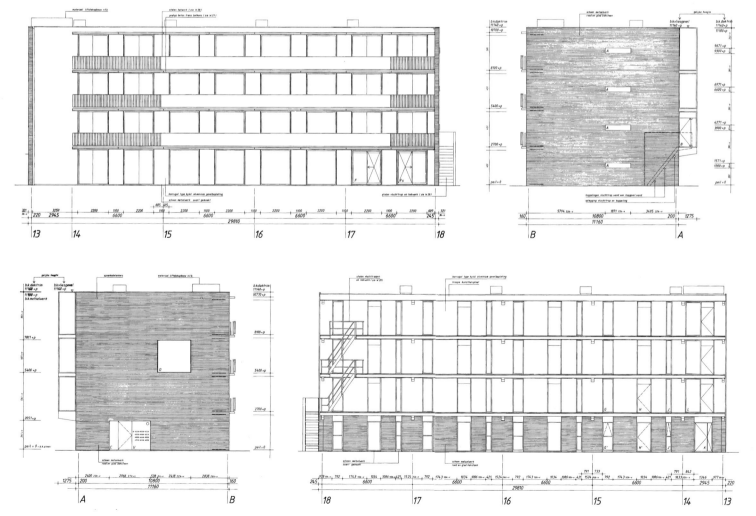

Elevations of C block

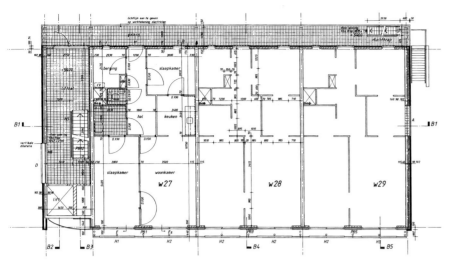

Plan of B block

The dwellings located in the apartment blocks are organised so that the kitchens and lobbies face the access gallery, whereas the bedrooms and living rooms face the green area.

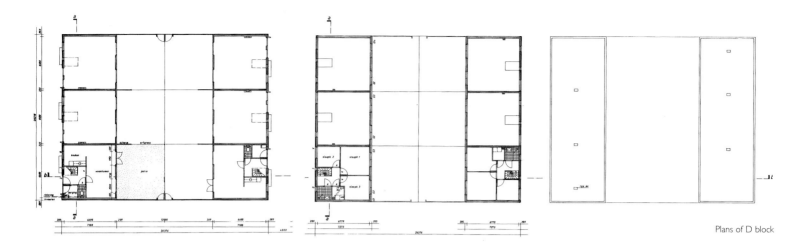

Plans of D block

The design and the materials used seek to create a deliberately abstract facade. Below, a view of the group of dwellings with courtyard.

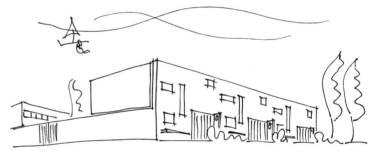

Maccreanor Lavington

Housing Project in Zaaneiland

Zaanstad, The Netherlands

This double strip of terraced housing plus an apartment building is situated on an island in a former industrial area 11 km from the centre of Amsterdam. It seeks to explore the transition space between the building and the public realm, the urban setting being more important than the perception of the buildings as discernible objects.

The bay-windowed living room offers a wide view over the promenade and the water. The windows and stairs act together as the main elements to define the transition between house and street. On the park side, the facades are noticeably shorter and a continuous garden zone forms an informal green space between the house and the park, the public park becoming a visual enlargement of the private green.

The apartment building has two very different elevations. The rear elevation is seen from the interior space between the terraced houses, and its design forms a closed brick ending to the mews. In contrast, the front of the building is only con-

cerned with its specific location on the edge of the island. Here the transparent elevation, consisting of large glazed balconies, overlooks the Zaan river as if quoting a seaside architecture. The glass facade consciously marks the transition from house to river landscape: from the inside it opens up towards the water and is conceived as a water-oriented extension of the living room. The monotone brick facades contribute to a sense of substance and wholeness, while the vertical rather than horizontal rhythms within the facade express the individuality of each house.

Typologically, the housing reflects a close connection between dwelling and car. The eastern terrace is raised to include a half-submerged internal garage. The importance of the street as a communicative space is further enhanced by the consciously street-orientated position of the raised living room, instilling a sense of control and security, opposing the tendency of retreat from the neighbourhood.

Photographs: Anne Bonsema

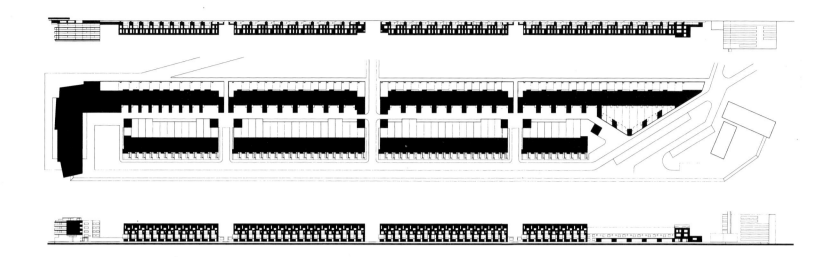

On this page, general ground plans, elevation and view of the residential complex with the block of apartments in the background.

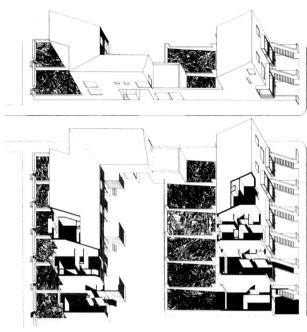

The facade of the row of dwellings is distinguished by the formal character of its openings and an entrance above ground level. The structuring of the dwellings in a row facilitates the creation of a hierarchy of streets and imposes a clear division between public, semi-public and private spaces.

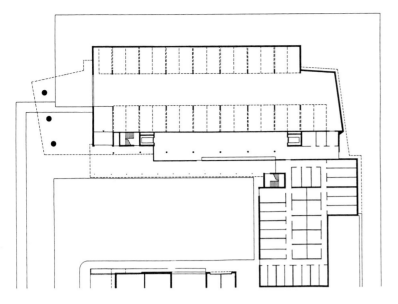

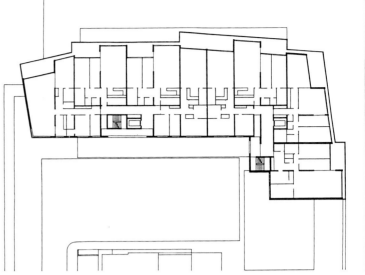

Ground floor plan of the apartment block

Typical floor plan of the apartment block

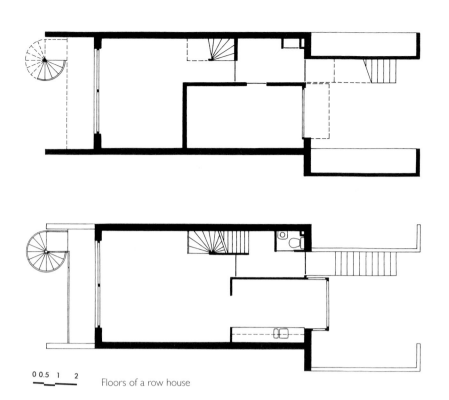
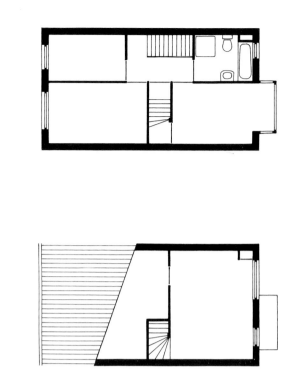

0 0.5 1 2

Floors of a row house

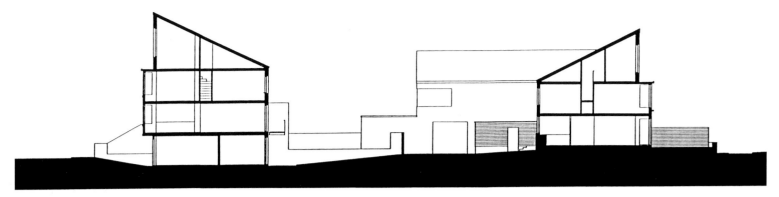

Cross-section of the terrace-houses

The uniformity of the continuous facades of exposed masonry helps to explain the project as a whole. On the other hand, the verticality marked by the rhythm of the openings expresses the individuality of each dwelling.

Geurst & Schulze Architekten

17 Residential Houses

De Aker, Amsterdam, The Netherlands

This project, situated in a residential area comprising some 3,200 dwellings, was developed in a former market-gardening area in Osdorp, Amsterdam.

This expansion area, "De Aker", is bounded on its southern edge by Haarlemmermeer's Ringvaart. The strip of luxury houses built following the design of Geurst & Schulze borders the drainage channel.

An important point of departure in the design was optimal privacy and freedom of choice in the use of various rooms. To this end, a difference in level has been created between the street and the drainage channel.

The living room is situated at a lower level, like a pavilion, on the water and is half the width of the house. By extending this part of the house to the water, the exterior space is screened off from the next-door house. The main volume is concentrated on the street side and is three storeys high. The sunken kitchen/dining-room, above which are the bedrooms, is situated on the street side. On the top storey there is a roof terrace which commands a view over the dike. The facades consist of large areas of white concrete blocks interspersed with slabs of dark concrete brick.

Photographs: PAC Rook

Perspective

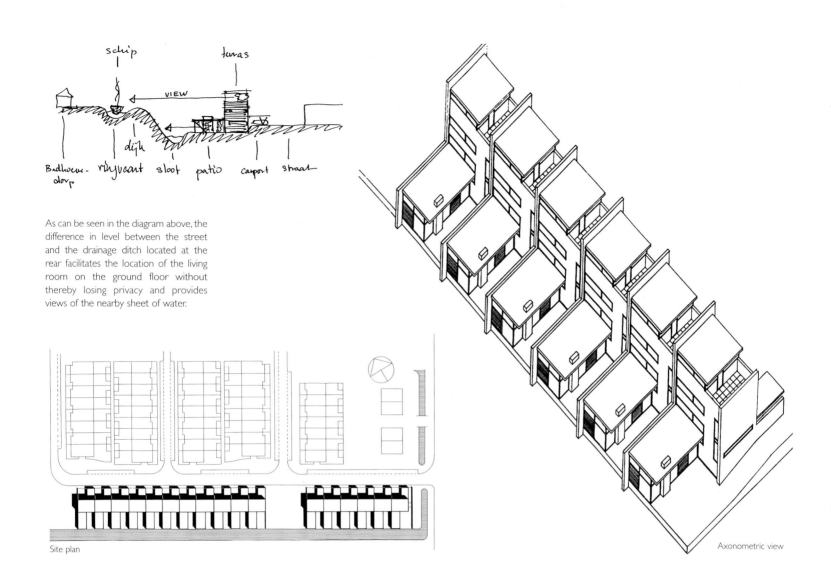

As can be seen in the diagram above, the difference in level between the street and the drainage ditch located at the rear facilitates the location of the living room on the ground floor without thereby losing privacy and provides views of the nearby sheet of water.

Site plan

Axonometric view

The composition of the facades arises from the interpolation of narrow strips of black between large areas of white, both made with prefabricated concrete blocks.

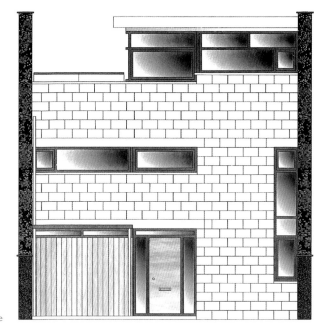

Garden and street facade

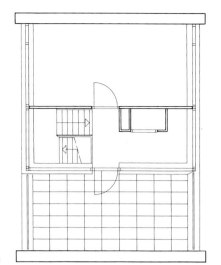

Upper level floor plan

First floor plan

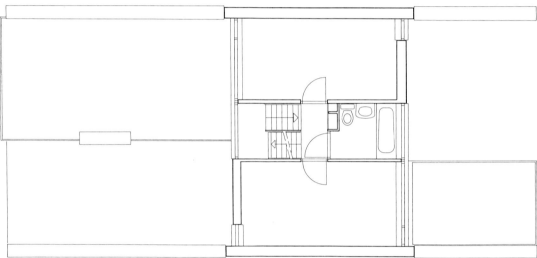

Ground floor plan

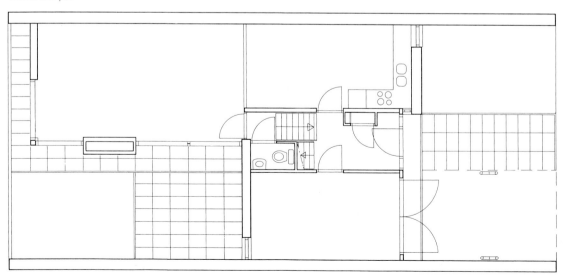

The entrance to the dwelling is marked by the presence of a simple structure of pure lines that protects the access area and defines the space of each dwelling visually.

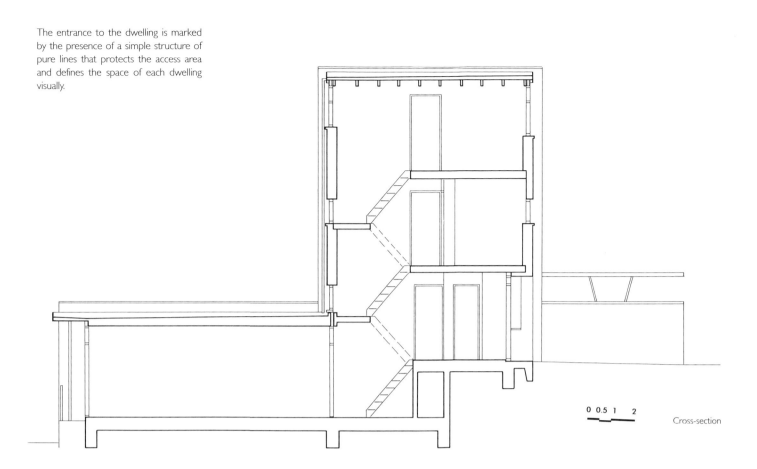

0 0.5 1 2

Cross-section

327

Schmidt, Hammer & Lassen

Thorninghøj Housing Scheme

Kolding, Denmark

The characteristic ring-shaped site plan, which the Thorninghøj housing scheme had to respect, was the result of a site plan competition in 1988. Thorninghøj consists of 65 housing units and a common house, which lies on the summit of the site at a junction of the municipal path system. The housing scheme is divided into four groups with two and three stories.

The units have direct exterior access from a common stairway to the first floor, where there is access to the units via a small stairway, as well as from suspended balcony corridors on the second floor with stairways at distinctive locations.

The buildings are built as large timber structures of oil-treated redwood, which in time will weather to a characteristic silver-grey.

All of the bays are of reddish-yellow, rough surfaced brick. The final colour harmony will be achieved when the facades are weathered.

The windows and doors are dark with distinctive ventilation grills in co-ordinated colours. The windows in the brickwork are painted white. All the buildings have broad eaves, which protect the balconies as well as the facades.

Photographs: Jens Nygaard

328

The buildings that form the housing complex were built using large structures of red sequoia wood treated with special oils for weather-resistance.

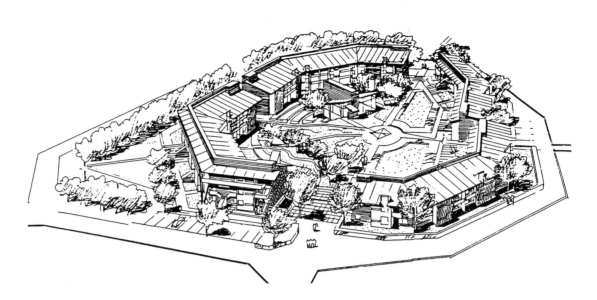

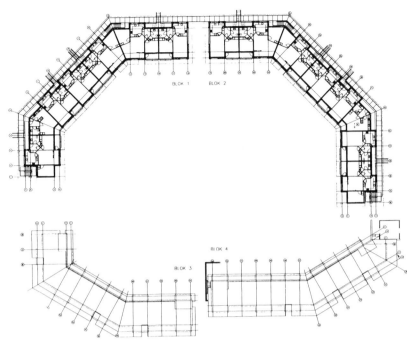

Standard floor plan

The windows and doors of the buildings were built in dark colours, with ventilation grilles in different colours. Everything is combined in harmony with the tone used for the wood on the exteriors.

All the buildings of the complex have wide eaves that were installed in order to protect the balconies and facade from the weather.

Typical plan of the apartments

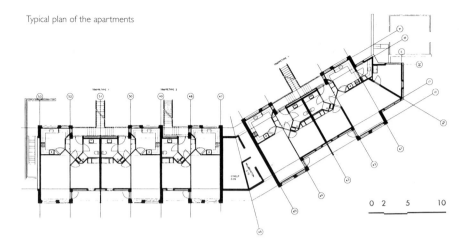

0 2   5   10

Each housing unit has direct access from the outside by a common staircase that goes up to the first floor. In the housing unit, with 65 units of two and three floors plus a common building, attention was paid to the interiors in consonance with the exterior.

Hans Kollhoff & Elga Timmermann

Malchower Weg

Berlin, Germany

The project, located in one of the first new residential districts in east Berlin, follows the line of compressing existing residential areas in order to restrict expansion at the periphery. It is also an attempt to bring urban refinement into an area that is shaped by prefabricated concrete buildings and country cottages.

The approximately square property has been divided and opened up through residential streets. The two blocks are raised 1.4 m and surrounded by a brick retaining wall creating a common garden area. A 90 cm high privet hedge provides the desired privacy. The design of the garden had to be simple and restrained, with a lawn and individual trees providing beautiful autumn colouring. Parking space is provided along the streets.

Facing the detached house development, the blocks are formed from 8 compact four-story buildings of 8 apartments each. The units are organised conventionally, each block being developed centrally; the ground plan is built symmetrically, creating a mirror image.

Value is placed on an agreeable, absolutely representative access area. The generous dimensioning of the stairwell, the wood panelling in the entrance area, the choice of a beautiful stone cladding, the handrails and entry doors to the flats in natural wood and a careful detailing ensure an atmosphere of quality.

On the outside the buildings have a conventional solid masonry with dark grouting, structured horizontally with prefabricated concrete strips. The windows are of natural wood. These unexceptional materials can age and keep maintenance costs low.

The flat sloping zinc roofs hang far out showing wooden eaves and give the houses the impression of security in surroundings that are today rather stark.

Photographs: Ulrich Schwarz

On the left, a view of the blocks from one of the inner courtyards. The exterior is characterised by the attractive texture of the wood frames and the exposed masonry walls framed by horizontal strips in reinforced concrete. A zinc roof with a generous overhang protects the blocks.

The blocks are raised from the street level by exposed masonry retaining walls. This improves the living conditions and the privacy of the ground floor flats. The garden was designed to be as simple as possible.

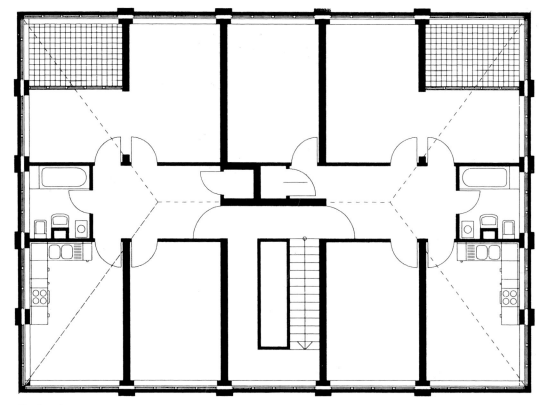

Top floor plan

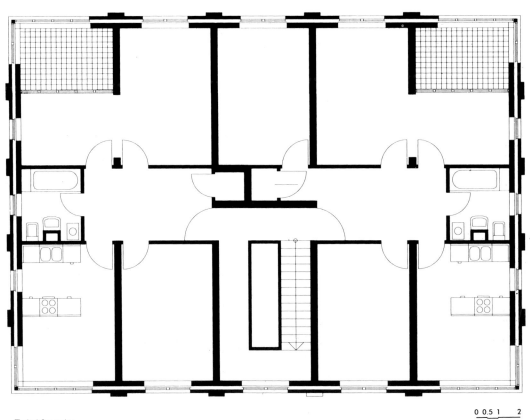

Typical floor plan

0 0.5 1   2

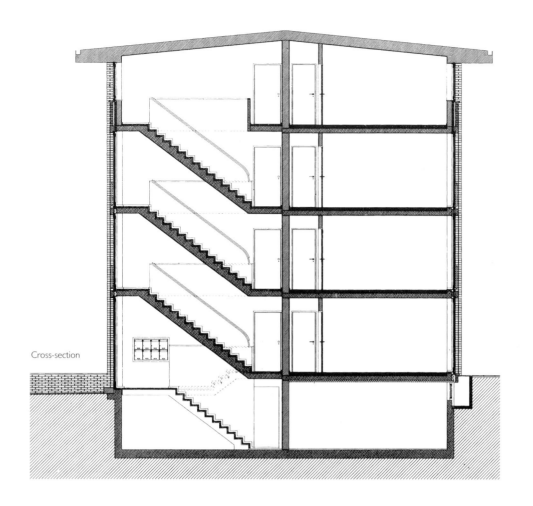

Cross-section

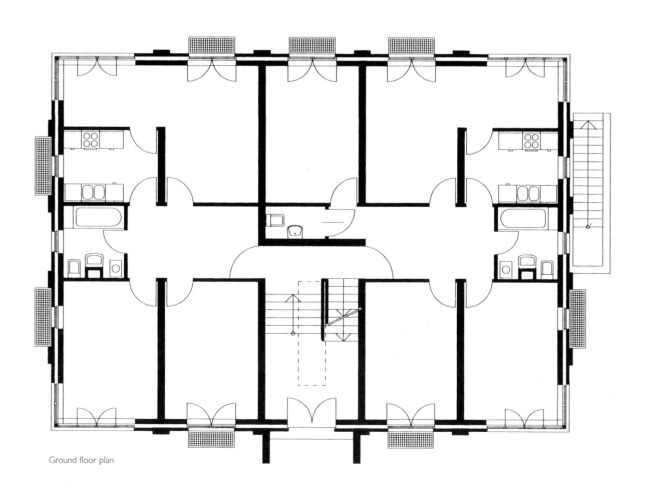

Ground floor plan

Entrance façade / *Fachada de ingreso*

Head of the complex / *Testero*

0 0 5 1   2

The complex is formed of sixteen blocks of four-floor dwellings. They are quite small though each one contains eight dwellings.

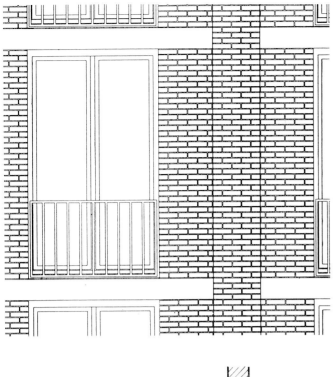

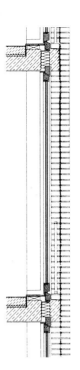

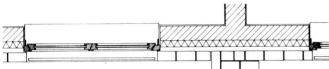

The exterior is characterised by the attractive texture of the wood frames and the expo-sed masonry walls framed by horizontal strips in rein-forced concrete. A zinc roof with a generous overhang protects the blocks. As can be seen in the picture bellow this caption, the common interior spaces are elegant and minimal.

Pasaje Santa Fe

México D.F., México

The building is located in the urban development of Santa Fe, which is the area of greatest development in Mexico City. The project is located in a zone called city centre, whose philosophy is to encourage pedestrian life and mixed use, mainly for housing, offices and shops.

The ground floor houses the commercial premises around a series of walkways, gardens and internal courts in order to encourage pedestrian life. Porticoes are used by the restaurants as terraces with tables.

The housing problem is becoming increasingly complicated in Mexico City due to the price of land. There are few options for young couples of the upper-middle to upper classes who were used to living in houses with a great deal of space and gardens. In the solution of Pasaje Santa Fe, though the apartments are small, the quality of life is not reduced.

62 apartments with an average size of 150 sqm. were built on the four upper levels. The apartments have two levels with spaces of double height that avoid the sensation of a traditional apartment. Different types of apartment were designed and each one has different views of the park or the interior terrace, or has balconies giving onto the street. Because it is a development aimed at young people, a cheerful image was sought for the building, with bright colours, fountains and gardens that differentiate the nature of the zones of the complex and do not give the impression of a traditional family block.

This type of project aims to recover the pedestrian and community life of the oldest neighbourhoods of the capital, which has been gradually lost in the new developments that are more influenced by the cities of the United States. Though little development work has been done in the zone so far, the results of this more human form of life, which offers greater quality of life, are beginning to be seen.

Photographs: Lourdes Legorreta

The housing complex is integrated into the urban layout and reflects confidence in a pedestrian ethic A series of passages, gardens and internal squares lend dignity to the project, which is defined by strong contrasts between volumes and colours.

1. Plaza
2. Store
3. Vegetation
4. Restaurant
5. PB Ground floor AP
5. PA Upper floor AP
A. Living room
B. Dining room
C. Kitchen
D. Bathroom
E. Master Bedroom
F. Bedroom
G. Maid room
H. Laundry
I. Dressing room
J. Toilet
K. Terrace
TP. Typical apartment

The buildings are developed around interior atriums with small gardens. The apartments have two levels with spaces of double height.

In his buildings, Legorreta always includes architectural features of great expressivity, such as the point of contact between the triangular wall and the porch. The result is a plastic play of light and shade that gives an added dimension to the unique distribution of the openings.

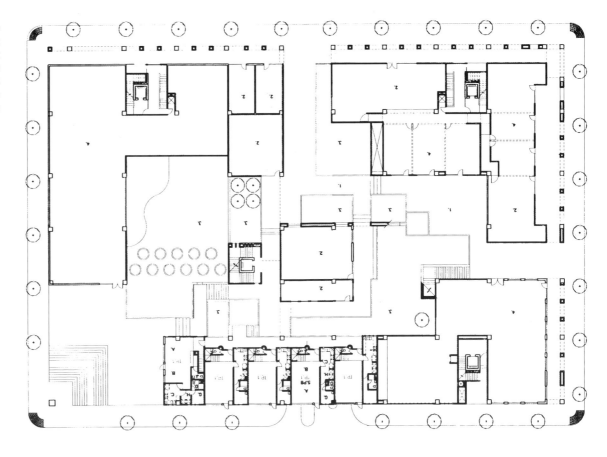

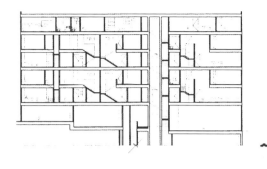

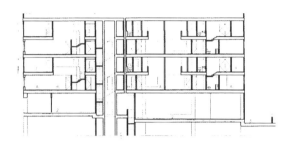

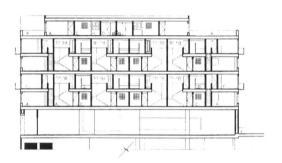

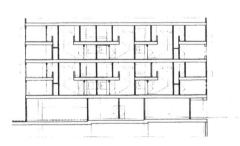

These pictures are clear examples of Legorreta's unique architectural idiom, composed of volume and colour, light and shade, presence and absence.
The access zones and internal corridors gain the benefit of landscaped areas that are strategically in tune with Legorreta's architecture.

K. Nikolaidis & C. Edwards

Apartments and Swimming pool

Santorini, Greece

This complex of 17 holiday apartments, with guest facilities and a swimming pool, was created amongst the existing, mostly subterranean houses of the village of Imerovigli, perched on the edge overlooking the volcanic landscape. The form of the complex evolves from a rational approach to the guest's needs, in conjunction with maximum use of the existing context and the addition of new, external buildings. Distinguished by the use of colour, the new structures follow the organisation of the existing buildings.

Particularly important in achieving the final result was the participation of local expert builders, thereby combining tradition with technology and modern materials.

The structure is spread over six levels that vary in height and overlap in many places. The second level accommodates the reception area, swimming pool, bar, dining and sitting areas, while the remaining levels are used for the apartments.

Entrance to the complex from the street is above level six, where a central staircase provides access to the four upper levels. This staircase then splinters to serve the pool/reception area and the apartments on the lower levels. In shaping the spaces, solutions were found which respected the lighting, the view and the privacy of all the apartments in the complex, in addition to those of the neighbouring buildings.

Bright colours are used for the complex, which correspond to the surroundings: earth, sea and sky are represented by ochre and brown, turquoise and azure, white and silver respectively. The selected materials are in keeping with those used previously for the site: the wooden doors and windows follow the same lines as those of the existing houses. External floors are made of rough cement. All visible timber is Swedish pine, employing a simple scaffold-like construction.

Photographs: D. Kalapodas & C. Edwards

346

West elevation

The new residential complex uses the original structure of the existing dwellings and transforms them into 17 semi-buried apartments set on the hillside and facing toward the sea.

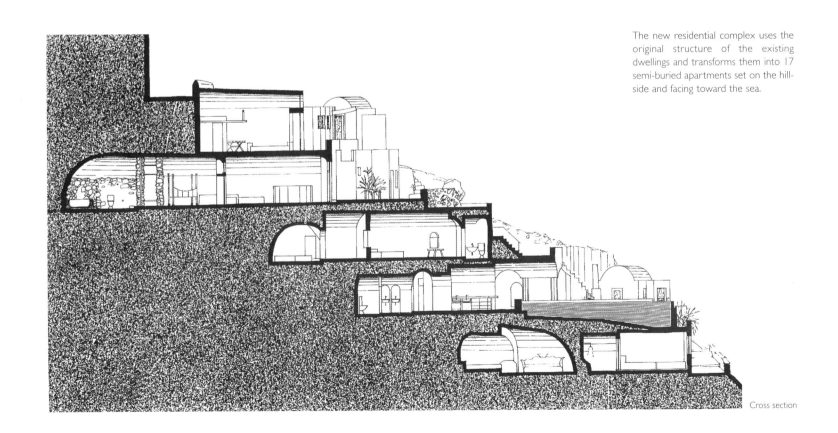

Cross section

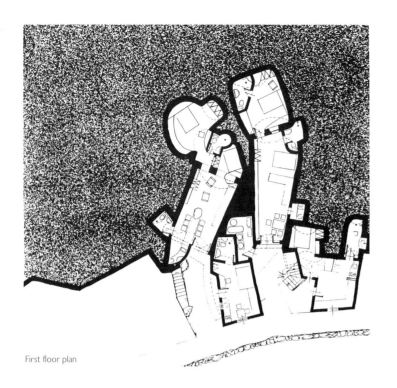

First floor plan

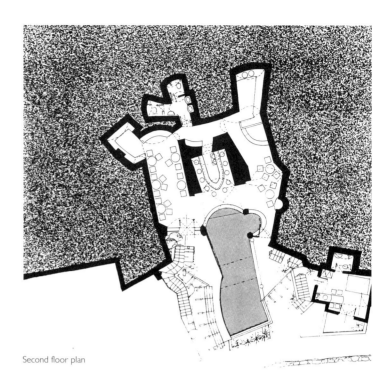

Second floor plan

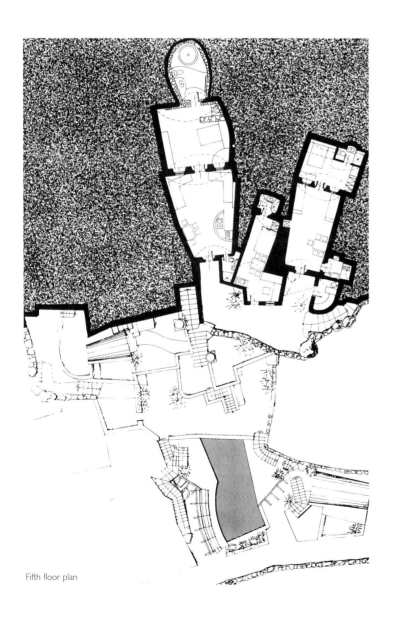

Fifth floor plan

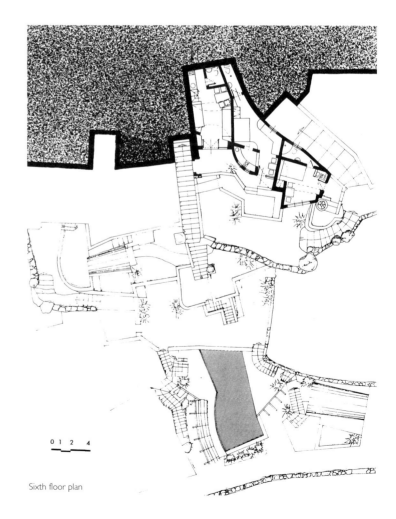

Sixth floor plan

0 1 2 4

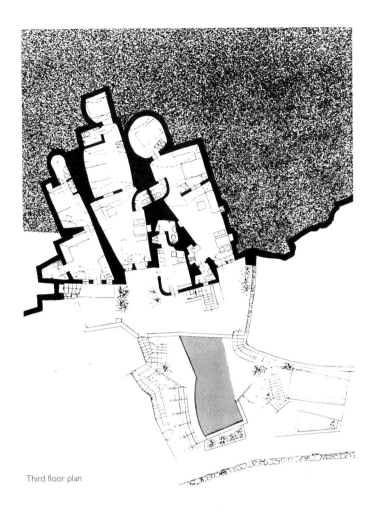

Third floor plan

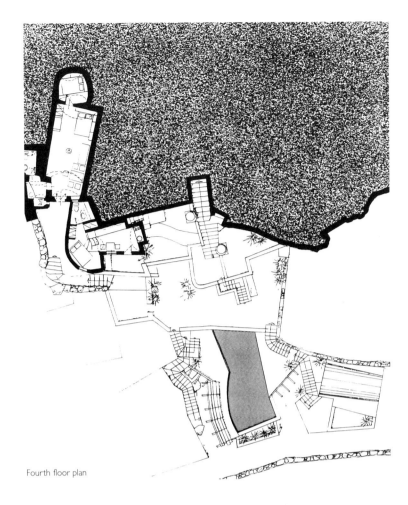

Fourth floor plan

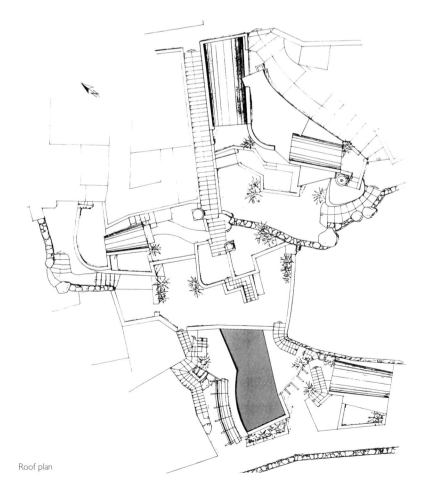

Roof plan

Deconstructivist and organic at the same time, the architecture of the complex uses the brilliant colours to emphasise its structure and to recompose the old elements following the local vernacular.

The partially covered swimming pool is located on the second floor and seems to be suspended from the hillside. A simple pine structure acts as a barrier defining the profile of the pool and serves as a seat.

The architects gave great importance to maintaining maximum privacy in the apartments, which are located on the first, third, fourth, fifth and sixth floors.

Bonell, Brullet, Gil & Rius
Centre Penitenciari de Brians

Sant Esteve de Sersovires, Spain

To build a prison is to build a closed world, like an abbey, a fortress, a monastery or an acropolis. Here life goes by in an absence of freedom. Relations are conditioned by control. There is a parallel with the ideas of the city. We find the same spaces as in the traditional city: squares, streets, facade. But the uses are not the same. Here, the square is not a place of meeting, but of classification. The street is not a place of communication, but of separation. The facade does not have the meaning of a relation between interior and exterior, but one of confinement.

The main features of these spaces are closed walls, passages, stairs, different levels and shadows. They are used in order to obtain variety and avoid monotony. Gestures and changes of alignment enrich and give greater meaning to a street that does not have the usual attributes such as windows and balconies.

The aim is to create a "city" on virgin land, paying attention to geo-graphical considerations and the landscape (good situation and integration) as well as the requirements, the latter being an aspect of great complexity in which questions of control and security take priority.

The requirements are satisfied by three clearly differentiated zones: The external zone, outside the walls, contains the administration services and is situated on the high part of the plot. On the other side of the wall we find the mixed zone, where the inmates are classified and where they make their contacts with the exterior: visits by relatives, lawyers, etc. From here we go into the internal zone containing residential modules, the hospital, the sports complex and the leisure areas, all located along a "street". This is the main axis of the penitentiary. A series of elements –the slope, the stairs, large overhangs, rotations, etc.– give value to a windowless facade and aid the effect of perspective.

Photographs: Lluis Casals

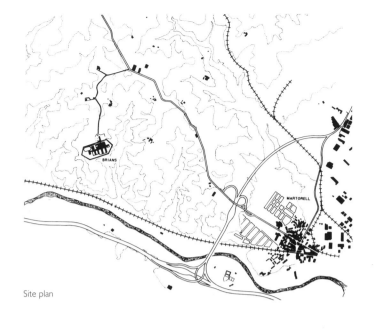

Site plan

Sketch

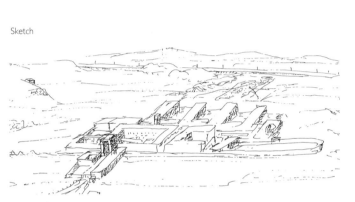

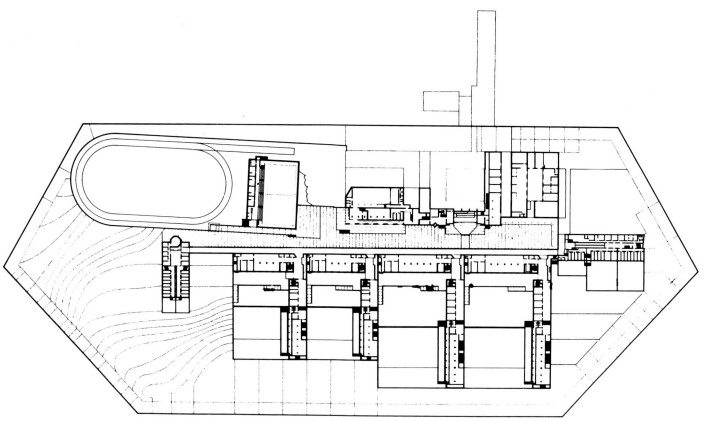

Floor at street level

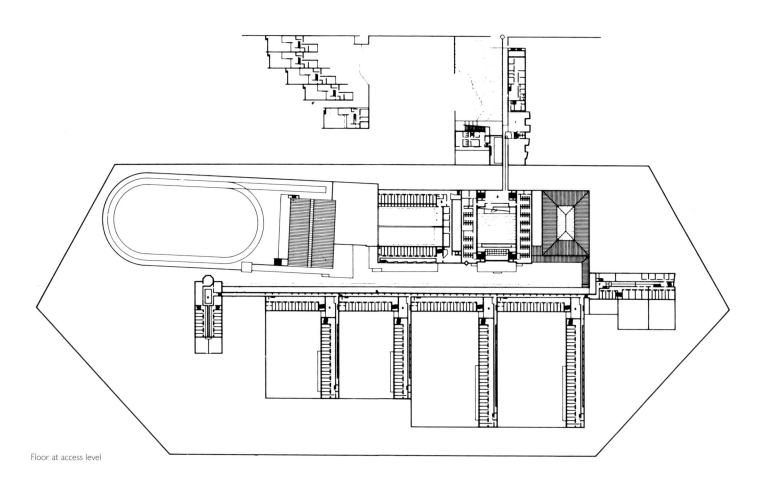

Floor at access level

Section D

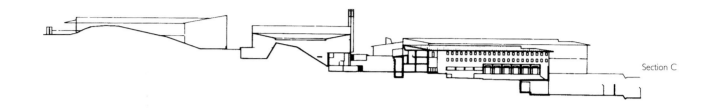

Section C

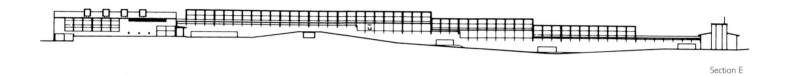

Section E

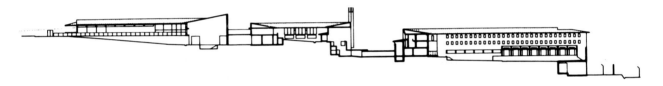

Section A

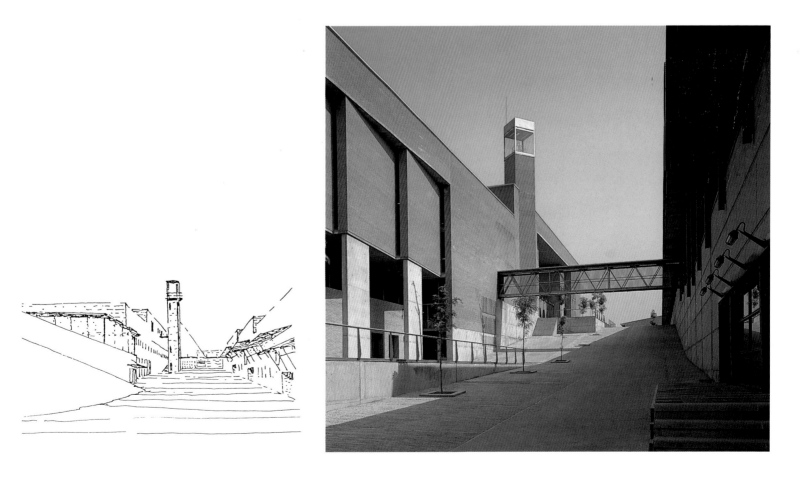

The design of the centre was based on a tripartite division: The extramural zone housing the administration services; the mixed zone used for visits and contacts with the exterior; and the internal zone housing the prison itself.

358

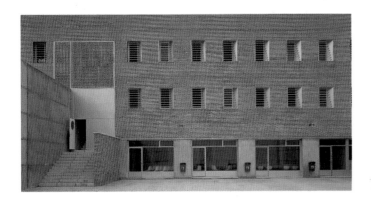

In order to avoid the monotony and exhaustive repetition that is habitual in this kind of centre, accidents and changes of alignment have been used: raised walkways, slopes…